JOE VALERIO
VALERIO DEWALT TRAIN

ARCHITECTURE

introduction by: **MALCOLM HOLZMAN**

RIZZOLI
NEW YORK

JOE VALERIO
VALERIO DEWALT TRAIN

for: JOE, ANTHONY, MARIAN, AND LINDA

First published in the United States of America in 1999 by
Rizzoli International Publications, Inc.
300 Park Avenue South
New York, NY 10010

Copyright © 1999
Rizzoli International Publications, Inc.

Library of Congress Cataloging-in-Publication Data

    Valerio, Joseph M.
        Joe Valerio of Valerio Dewalt Train Associates /
        foreward by Malcolm Holzman.
               p.   cm.
        Includes bibliographical references.
        ISBN 0-8478-2171-4 (pbk.)
        1. Valerio, Joseph M.—Themes, motives—Exhibitions.
        2. Modernism (Art)—United States—Influence—Exhibitions.
        I. Title. II. NA737.V355A4 1999
        720'.92—dc21 98-48809
                              CIP

Graphic Design by Kasia Gawlik Parker

Printed and bound in Hong Kong

PHOTO CREDITS

THIS PAGE: Detail of Support Pod in the Unet Manufacturing Facility. Photo by Barbara Karant of Karant + Associates, Chicago, Illinois.

FRONT COVER: Colton Palms Apartments, photo by Barbara Karant of Karant + Associates, Chicago, Illinois.

PAGE 160: Drawing of the Gardner Apartment Stair.

BACK COVER UPPER: Colton Palms Apartments, photo by Barbara Karant of Karant + Associates, Chicago, Illinois.

BACK COVER LOWER: Gardner Apartment, photo by Barbara Karant of Karant + Associates, Chicago, Illinois.

ACKNOWLEDGMENTS

Architecture is both intentional and accidental. Each of the illustrated buildings is the final line in a highly complex script which began in some cases as early as the 1960s. Each represents the contribution of collaborators including Linda Searl, and associates in Chrysalis, Valerio Associates, and Valerio Dewalt Train. Of equal importance is the collaboration with the owners of these buildings. Often their willingness to be players taking a chance on something novel and unruly encouraged invention. The first people who were willing to suspend their disbelief were teachers at the University of Michigan and the University of California, Los Angeles. The most recent is David Morton, whose thoughtful editing is a major contribution to this work.

In between, many people affected and contributed to both the thought and the substance of the work. In some cases the collaboration was active, while in other cases it was passive. Some people affected every building while in other cases they played a role in only one. They share in common an appreciation for a design which reflects thoughtful planning and unexpected benefits of pure chance.

The "afterwards" recognizes collaborating architects from Chrysalis, Valerio Associates, and Valerio Dewalt Train. Other people who have made a critical contribution include:

Phil Alongi, *NBC News*
Marvin Adelson, *UCLA*
Robert Beckley, *University of Michigan*
Frank Benest, *City of Colton*
Brad Binkowski, *Urban Land Interests*
Casey Cowell, *U.S. Robotics Corporation*
Mike Davies, *Chrysalis Corporation*
Robert Darvas, *University of Michigan*
Abe Darwish, *3Com Corporation*
Neal David, *Lincoln Park Zoological Society*
Chris Dawson, *Chrysalis Corporation*
John Morris Dixon, *Progressive Architecture*
Steve Dragos, *Milwaukee Redevelopment Corporation*
Tom Drilias, *Summerfest*
Tim and Suzette Flood
Richard Friedman, *U.S. Robotics and 3Com Corporation*
Tracy Gardner
Katie, David and Annie Gingrass
Bob Greenstreet, *University of Wisconsin— Milwaukee*
Gary and Carol Griffith
David Hall, *U.S. Robotics Corporation*
Thomas and Maxine Herz
Kent Hubbell, *Chrysalis Corporation*
Alex Jackson, *Carnegie Art Institute*
Mickey Kupperman, *A. Epstein & Sons International, Inc.*
Susan Grant Lewin
Roland Lieber, *Swanke Hayden Connell Architects*
Randall Marmor
Richard Marmor, *Arbour Development Company*
Jim Murphy, *Progressive Architecture*
Tom Neujahr, *Urban Land Interests*
Harvey Perloff, *UCLA*
Keith and Rose Lee Reinhard
Gabe Reisner, *WMA Consulting Engineers, Ltd.*
Liz Ryan, *U.S. Robotics Corporation*
Ron Saks, *LMI Aerospace*
Roger Schluntz, *Arizona State University*
Darwin Smith, *Kimberly Clark Corporation*
Alan Stanton, *Chrysalis Corporation*
Karen Stein, *Architectural Record*
Jennifer Thornberry, *City of Colton*
Fred Wood, *Cooperative Services, Inc.*

Critical to understanding the architecture in this book is the transformation of a three-dimensional experience to a two-dimensional photograph. For the most part these transformations reflect the partnership between Joe Valerio as architect and Barbara Karant as photographer. Her talent has always been to use the experience of the building as the substance of her art.

And lastly, to a great degree this book is the invention of Kasia Gawlik Parker who was responsible for the design and contributed greatly to the essays. ∎

CONTENTS

buildings & designs continued

INTRODUCTION

BY MALCOLM HOLZMAN

Architecture is the most public of all art forms. It is ironic that its initial conception is a solitary process. Ultimately, to achieve a completed project, architecture requires collaboration with clients, contractors, business associates, and many other individuals. But the source of a design is always attributable to one individual, who, with a specific series of ideas and images, offers a private vision. This publication of images and words provides insight to Joe Valerio's secret moments.

Chicago, the city of the big shoulders, has been strongly identified with architectural firms that integrate design and business—Burnham & Root, Adler & Sullivan, Skidmore Owings & Merrill, Murphy/Jahn—all produced iconic buildings with which we are quite familiar. Their practices were based on the concept of a designer whose talents combined with the abilities of others to construct complex projects. For the last half dozen years, Valerio Dewalt Train has operated in this typical Chicago tradition. Jack Train is no longer active in the firm; Mark Dewalt manages the business side, which Chicagoans understand is crucial to producing projects of excellence; Joe Valerio is responsible for design. He came to this understanding of the architectural business in his hometown by taking a circuitous path: from Chicago to California to Washington to Milwaukee, he browsed through other conventions of practice, only to return home to Chicago as the firm's designer. His travels provided insight and experience to establish Valerio Dewalt Train within the Chicago prescription for success—an acceptable organizational structure which allows for freedom of design expression.

Valerio's current design work is not the result of a sudden awakening in a new environment. Rather, he has carried forward a distinct individuality that continues to renounce the pedestrian charms of popular design styles for the exploration of his own private beliefs. Architects attain their goals in invidious ways. Being no exception, Valerio does so by parlaying his talent outside the context of the work at hand.

Since his firm is engaged in the commerce of construction, a divergent range (residential, religious, commercial, etc.) of projects emerges. Starting with more or less conventional owner requirements, their final appearance bespeaks a transcendent design formula. Mostly modern, but romantically abstract with a reductionist appearance, they are the result of an accumulated vocabulary finely honed from three decades of work.

All architects devise strategies to organize their projects. Some rely on the tried and true; others invent their own. Valerio uses a variety of them. But there is one key strategy Valerio employs in almost every undertaking that connects all the building projects together and gives them his imprint. Any one project may not on its own appear to provide evidence of this method. Only when a group of projects are seen together does it become apparent. Valerio is interested in sequential arrangements of objects. From project to project, the set of organized items will vary so that seldom is the same element manipulated in the same way twice. Most frequently he will take one of the parts of a building then group them in a special order. Sloping columns, triangular panels, stair treads, and risers have all been employed as part of this strategy.

Modernists used structure, functionalists used mechanical systems; Valerio employs the repetition of distinct elements to provide a focus in his work. They become a method to define a space, a circulation pattern, or a specific form. The "V" columns and circular openings in the Dream House provide a limit for the residence's enclosure; the Griffith House replicates an ordinary wood-frame house to double its size; and columns placed at the intersection of the orthogonal circulation plan of the U2 Manufacturing Facility are obvious examples of this strategy. Mastery of this technique has led to inverted variations: on the facade of the Pillsbury Research and Development Headquarters, large wall panels alternate with columns. First the columns are on the bottom, in the next segment they are on top, changing places with the panels. In the center of the Opera House Restaurant the upper enclosure of the bar is sheathed in veneered wood panels: each triangular panel alternates with the next; first the base is at the bottom and then the apex, next followed by a base. This clever arrangement also allows for the depiction of a large oval with flat panels. Seeing this technique employed so frequently can also imply that it is being used even when there is no repetition: the two boxes of the Gardner Apartment, located on the fifty-eighth and fifty-ninth floors above Michigan Avenue, can be viewed as a quirky example of the alternation method—a metal box followed by a wood box, a gridded box playing against a box with curves. It is tacitly understood that if the apartment were ever to expand upwards, the next levels would follow this alternating sequence.

All architects order their work. It is only with the assemblage of all these Valerio projects within the two covers of a book that this organizing device becomes legible. In an era when ambiguity and chaos have held great interest for designers, it is rewarding to see beyond the surface gloss to the arranged workings of one architect's inner methods. Seeing and understanding Valerio's sequential ordering device does not diminish his architecture. Nor does it make for boring and predictable buildings. In fact, they remind me of the very popular children's book *Where's Waldo?* Searching through his work for an arranged pattern—be it repetition, consecution, or alternation—only adds more pleasure and delight to the viewing. ∎

UNEXPECTED ARCHITECTURE

BY JOE VALERIO

*. . . One of the ways in which American
experience liberated the New World was by
freeing men from the notion that every grand
institution needed a grand foundation of
systematic thought: that successful government
had to be supported by profound political theory,
that moving religion had to be supported by
subtle theology—in a word, that the best living
had to have behind it the most sophisticated
thinking. This mood was to explain the superficially
contradictory strains of the practical and traditional
in the American mind—the openness to novel ways
that worked and the readiness to accept ancient and
traditional laws—for both common sense and common
law were time-proven and unreflective ways of
settling problems.*

*In America what seemed to be needed was
not so much a new variant of European "schools"
of philosophy as a philosophy of the unexpected.
Too much of the best-elaborated thinking of the
European mind added up to proof that America and
its novelties were impossible. A less aristocratic
and more mobile New World required a way of
interpreting experience that would be ready for
the outlandish and would be equally available to
everyone everywhere.*[1]

DANIEL J. BOORSTIN

▲ *A basketball court at the end of the Homer Township subdivision in the Chicago area. The image is from a "Nation of Strangers" published in the* Chicago Tribune *in the last week of December, 1995. Chicago Tribune photo by Bill Hogan.*

Innovation in architecture is an act of civil disobedience. Defying expectations and uprooting accepted norms, the visually wayward building ignores the natural complacency of the American architectural landscape. This visual inertia is a stylistic shorthand representing traditional, comfortable, convenient associations with the past. The consequences of severing this connection can be painful—derision, ridicule, and, worst of all, laughter. The architect's willingness to take risks is increased if people have an openness to novel solutions.

If in the past a culture was expected to offer a systematic view of the world, then in the U.S. contradictions are more the norm. Anything expected seems curiously inappropriate. In Chicago, there are old neighborhoods for newcomers, new suburbs for those who have lived in the city for a while, and a downtown that everyone shares. It is a place long on practical experience, but short on theories and philosophies. An architecture appropriate for Chicago would reflect very shallow traditions and a very deep respect for the individual experiences that have formed its visual landscape.

In Chicago, like most U.S. cities, architecture is contradictory: it is alternately comfortable and cheap, convenient and ugly, historic and repressive, innovative and threatening. Ordinarily, architects experience little pressure from clients to fit a building into the overall context.

Practical experience, convenience, and economics drive the design of the built environment in America. Dressed up in vinyl siding, the stick-built,

▲ *A patch of blue sky framed by three adjacent buildings in Arbour Park Apartments in Tempe, Arizona.*

dingbat apartment building is undeniably comfortable, but not necessarily beautiful. The automobile and the desire for convenience have created the minimall. Evolved from the corner store, the strip mall's storefronts have moved back from the sidewalk to allow room for customers to park their cars. Each store's hyperactive signage is brighter, louder, and larger than its predecessor's to catch the attention of potential customers driving past. Both the minimall and its ancestor coexist on the same street.

Only with substantial effort can consistency displace convenience. For instance, the Disney-built town of Celebration in Florida is remarkably systematic. Its imagery has been codified in a pattern book required

to be used by all homebuilders. Style is law, limiting individual choice and possibly delaying the addition of a room, the installation of a satellite dish, or any number of other conveniences in each owner's home. Apparently absent in this ideal suburb, with its perfectly proportional houses, each with the requisite porch, are any visible contradictions. No vices, even minor ones, are in evidence; there is nothing outlandish nor is there any sense that this ideal place could be available to everyone.

Yet hidden behind the approved facades, contradictions exist. Celebration's architecture alludes to a familiar past while its town plan does not. The high school is adjacent to the city center. The downtown buildings are donut shaped, not to create courtyards or atria, but to hide the conveniently located parking area and maintain the carefully produced image of a traditional street front. Lastly, while real estate prescribes that houses of different cost cannot share the same street, the designers of Celebration have provided yet another innovation: larger homes share the same alley with less expensive ones.

The significance placed on individual choice illustrates how people can accept change without a great sense of loss. Convenience justifies both maintaining and departing from the expected way of doing things. Entire new building typologies, such as the supermarket, are defined, accepted, and made the norm, with little regard for the small, personalized shops and stores that were replaced. Convention is not sacred.

The prevailing mode is to accept change, then explain it. Something new does not have to be seen as part of a larger whole, it simply has to work. This condition impacts almost everything, including buildings. In the past, architecture was expected to be a measure of culture as a whole—defining, explaining, and making a place understandable. Today, in the United States, where the whole is made up of many unexplained and unexpected things, architecture has become equally unexpected and contradictory.

If architecture is a measure of culture, what architecture can measure this culture? Each of the following eight chapters "takes the temperature" of the U.S. and then draws connections between those observations and the work of different artists and architects, including ourselves. These thoughts do not attempt to prove anything; they are only intended to raise suspicions. Organized into two groups, the first set—Leaving,

Pressure, Rootlessness, History Is Over—look backward, documenting a series of observations about American culture. The second set—Innocence, Comfort: A Guilty Pleasure, Self-Evidence, Ambiguity of the Missing Narrative—look forward, defining these four aspects of contemporary American architecture. The observations and opinions in these chapters are all afterthoughts, reflections on the initial intent of architecture, which is transformed by the design process and only becomes a fully formed idea after a building is complete. ■

From the beginning, Americans formed a habit of accepting for the most part only those ideas which seemed already to have proved themselves in experience. They used things as they were as a measure of how things ought to be; in American the "is" became the yardstick of the "ought." Was not the New World a living denial of the old sharp distinction between the world as it might be or ought to be?[2]

DANIEL J. BOORSTIN

LEAVING   PRESSURE   ROOTLESS   HISTORY IS OVER

LEAVING   PRESSURE   ROOTLESS   HISTORY IS OVER

Of all the things we observe, only a small portion will be remembered. Some of these observations recur over and over, becoming the foundation for our buildings. The first four chapters—LEAVING, PRESSURE, ROOTLESS, and HISTORY IS OVER—make note of these recurring observations. The associated buildings are reflections of these observations.

▲ Untitled Film Still #48, by Cindy Sherman, 1979. Courtesy the artist and Metro Pictures.

American architecture,

will mean, if it ever succeeds

in meaning anything,

American life.[1]

LOUIS H. SULLIVAN

The woman in Cindy Sherman's *Untitled Film Still #48* appears to be leaving as she stands by the edge of the highway, a suitcase by her side, the two-lane road curving out of sight to the left. The photograph could mean anything; the content is ambiguous. The image invites a narrative; she waits for a bus to take her away, she goes willingly, innocence about to be lost. Maybe she is a symbol for all of us who have left everything behind.

Where is she going? Is she just another girl leaving for the city? The city often symbolizes risk in films, places where the bonds to the comforts of the past are broken. Cities are lonely places where individuals can only depend on themselves, without the help of family or community.

The thing she leaves behind may be a comfortable town or small farm. The idealized images of these places come to mind. By leaving, she separates herself from the land, from the community, from the shared languages of the past. The nonverbal languages of buildings, clothing, and other things long accepted are also questioned. The integrity of this comfortable fabric

of thoughts is at risk as she stands alone by the side of the road.

Before she left, she did not think of herself as an individual. Now, she is on her own. Through the immigrant experience, the comforts of the old community are lost. Although naive, she gains confidence as she gains experience. It is all part of that favorite myth of film scripts—experience outweighs the value of all other forms of education. Leaving the security and comfort of the past behind, people are successful by first observing and then innovating. It is a familiar trade-off in films; the comfort of conforming to the norms of the community is exchanged for the risks and opportunities of individual freedom.

The Viennese architect Adolf Loos wrote in "Ornament and Crime" in 1908:

> *Primitive men had to differentiate themselves by*
> *various colours, modern man needs his clothes as*
> *a mask. His individuality is so strong that it can*
> *no longer be expressed in terms of items of*
> *clothing. The lack of ornament is a sign of intel-*
> *lectual power. Modern man uses the ornament of*

past and foreign cultures at his discretion. His own
inventions are concentrated on other things.[2]

Loos saw modernization as freeing the individual to innovate. The traditions of fashion are used or they are discarded. Dress is a matter of individual choice, not of community mores. By extension, architecture is also a matter of individual choice. Such choices change the way we think of a place.

Traditionally, internally consistent cultures are usually defined by a particular place. A consistent architecture of common materials is used to build towns where everything from the pattern of the streets to the shape of the windows reminds people of a certain shared history. Often a single building serves as a landmark for an entire town. Certain places refresh the community's memories of a common past. These memories make it possible to reach common interpretations about almost anything, from the cut of a jacket to the form of a building. But once accepted, these memories make it difficult for a homogeneous community to accept innovation and agree on change.

As a result of migrating to the U.S., the heterogeneous population remembers different places and different histories. Almost immediately memories begin to fade, old places are inaccurately remembered, and the fabric of history wears thin. Yet people are creatures of habit, they still want to find and understand the underlying ideas that govern the shape of things. They understand that something has been forgotten.

Where communities of people were once spectators recalling established traditions, the fading and no longer shared memories make people individual participants in a volatile and often contradictory competition of ideas. Buildings are part of this competition. One building can be replaced by another as easily as one TV channel is changed for another. What is becomes what ought to be, until it is replaced and ultimately forgotten. Place no longer matters as it once did. In this atmosphere, established rules can be tested, and civil disobedience in all its forms becomes less risky. Individuals can accept innovation more easily than the larger community. When convenient, traditions that still work remain in place, while others that do not can easily be discarded. The rule of convenience accepts both the most innovative building and, at the same time, traditional architecture. Both can coexist without any need to explain the evident contradictions.

The picturesque suburb attempts to dampen the speed of change by making the newly minted towns of the twentieth-century U.S. become more like the comfortable small towns of pre-modern America. Banning contradictions is the objective of Celebration, Florida. But such communities and the expectations on which they are founded cannot be sustained against even the mildest forms of civil disobedience. Herbert Muschamp in his *New York Times* review of "The American Lawn: Surface of Everyday Life" at the Canadian Centre for Architecture observed "Since cultural values tend to coax up their opposites, a space dedicated to harmony and independence can easily become a battlefield. Is the overgrown lawn a protected form of speech? How about Christmas ornaments on the lawn? Or a cross-burning?"[3] With the first outrageous act of the disobedient individual, the system begins to wobble out of control. With the first unruly lawn, the speed of change increases, leaving the past behind. ■

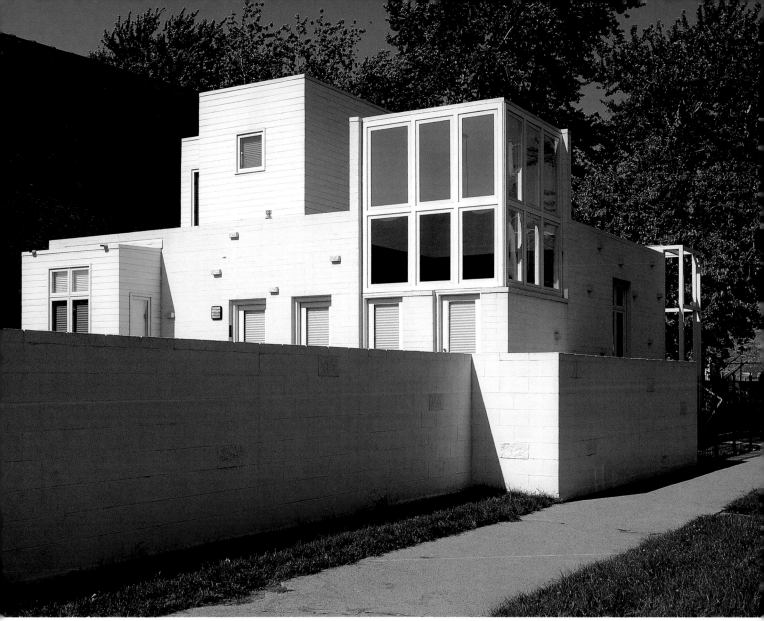

▲ *The south elevation as seen from the sidewalk on Oakley Boulevard.*

◄ *The two front doors of the Ohio House, both leading to the same room.*

OHIO HOUSE

designed jointly with
Linda Searl
client
Joe Valerio and Linda Searl
site
Chicago, Illinois
completed
1989

Cities are for the most part streets. They are gathering places for the community, sometimes filled with tension, sometimes violence. City streets are everything that suburban streets are not. After all, they are still used for something other than reaching a garage. What happens on city streets is always unpredictable and unexpected, especially on the street corner.

On the corner of Ohio Street and Oakley Boulevard, in Chicago's Ukranian Village, resides the Ohio House, which was designed by and for the architect and his wife, Linda Searl.

The design conceit begins with a simple white box. White masonry walls define a square plan enclosing 1,700 square feet of living space. Open or glass-enclosed frameworks raise and extend each corner of the box. Unexpectedly, the building expands at the corners, while the center of each facade recedes. The entry is located at the implied intersection of two of the masonry planes, instead of at the center of either one. Rather than one front door, there are two—one facing each

▲ The north elevation facing Ohio Street.

▲ The kitchen window looking past the adjacent apartment building toward Ohio Street.

▲ The dining room is separated from the kitchen by stacked storage cabinets.

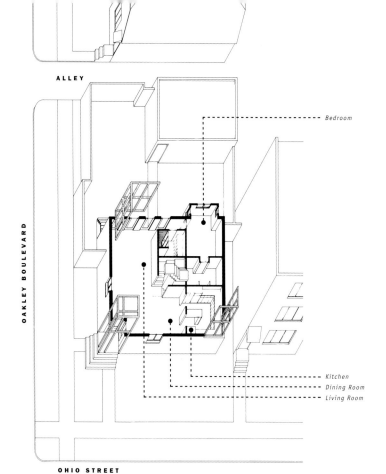

ALLEY

OAKLEY BOULEVARD

Bedroom

Kitchen
Dining Room
Living Room

OHIO STREET

north, FIRST FLOOR PLAN not to scale.

street. The conventional hierarchy of a house is intentionally reversed. The mass of the building is denied.

Within the house, the most public elements of the plan run parallel to either street—the living room is aligned with Oakley, bending to form the dining room/kitchen paralleling Ohio Street. At the inside corner of this L defined by these two rooms is the internal stair connecting the first floor with the basement and upstairs study. The stair is also at the center of the house's nine-square plan. The most private functions occupy the corner furthest from the street.

The composition of the house is not settled, like the corner of Ohio and Oakley streets, a favored gathering place for different people. The local street gangs—who regularly mark the red brick houses in the neighborhood, but not the white walls of the Ohio House—meet on this corner. The ice-cream vendor stops here every evening. The Jehovah's Witnesses choose this corner to start their rounds on Sundays. Both the corner and the house are open to interpretation, "used" by many different people in very different ways. ■

▲ A glass-enclosed framework extends the space of the living room corner skyward.

OHIO HOUSE ADDITION

designed jointly with
Linda Searl
client
Joe Valerio and Linda Searl
site
Chicago, Illinois
completed
1999

The corner of Ohio and Oakley has changed little since the construction of the Ohio House. In the intervening nine years the two industrial loft buildings on the northeast and northwest corners have been renovated as loft apartments. For the most part they appear the same except for new windows.

Just when the neighborhood is getting use to the white house on the corner, a new second and third floor are being added. An aluminum cylinder is taking shape on top of the original square masonry base. The circular form is truncated along the interior wall of the living room, leaving a flat rectangular surface facing east. The large monitor window over the stair is at the center of this surface. Overlooking Ohio Street the third-floor bedroom cantilevers from this facade appearing as an aluminum and glass cube. A second box with a clerestory over the third-floor bath balances on the edge of the parapet.

The white walls and cubic forms of the Ohio House were an unruly addition to the corner of Ohio and Oakley. Although unexpected, it has been accepted. The curved addition is a new idea layered on an older one, like a new character added to street's soap opera. ■

▲ *The aluminum-skinned addition as seen from the corner of Ohio and Oakley adds two levels to the house. The cantilevered box is a third-floor bedroom.*

LEAVING

IN-BETWEEN HOUSE

client
Pacific-Sakata Development, Inc.
site
Burr Ridge, Illinois
designed
1991

Seiji Suzuki is the developer of Falling Water, a speculative land development of some two hundred home sites in the Chicago area. Born and raised in Japan, Seiji, now thirty-eight years old, came to America when he was nineteen.

Half there, half here, Seiji has a vague conviction that the suburban house is somehow disconnected from both the city and the land, a problem which he sensed Frank Lloyd Wright was trying to mend. The name Falling Water is a homage to this effort. To make his point, Seiji commissioned eight architects to design medium-sized houses to be built on different homesites in his hilly, tree-covered development. The development is a joint venture between Pacific Planning and Sakata Construction Company, the fourth largest construction company in Japan.

Each design was for sale to purchasers of a home site. These homebuyers are part of an ongoing migration from city to suburb, from suburb to suburb, wishfully looking for that last stop. For most people, there is the vague, often inaccurate atavistic memory of leaving an idealized agrarian existence for life in the city; their intention is to return to the country, and instead they wind up in the suburbs. Supporting the illu-

sion is the suburban house intended to be the "country house." It is a fantasy about what we were, instead of a reflection of what we are. Attempting a course correction, leaving the notion of the suburban house behind, the eight designs try to reconnect the land and the city. Of course, none of the designs ever sold.

The In-Between House is an allegory about the ironies of escaping to the suburbs. At one end, the house is anchored to the city by something that looks vaguely like a skyscraper. Purposely unspecific yet familiar, the tower embraces bigness. At the opposite end of the house, a sunken courtyard captures a bit of idealized nature within its walls. In between these two opposites is the house, touching the city on one end, and brushing up against a man-made interpretation of nature. Real nature, with all of its dangers and primitive goings-on, can be safely glimpsed in the surrounding forest through the openings in the garden wall.

This interpretation reflects only one view. There is false comfort in the obvious—the building that appears to be about a single idea. The In-Between House is not supposed to offer obvious or simple explanations. There are other things going on. The communal spaces are arranged on a single

elevated plane; below this deck are the bedrooms, each reached by a separate stair. Two paths run through the house. One winds up and through all the family spaces; it is not direct and the destination is never clear. A second exterior path along the back wall moves up a straight, shallow stair emerging on a bridge, which leads to a elliptical stair descending to the garden. Each path offers different ways to experience the same idea. There is surprising comfort in a building that can be interpreted and used in a number of unexpected ways. ■

▲ *Looking up toward the house from the forest below.*

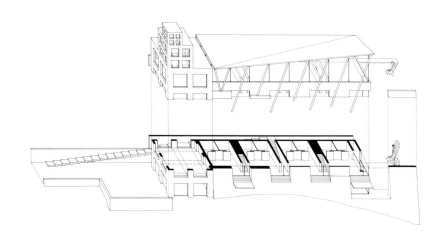

◀ The form of the living room implies
a building from the city.

▶ The front door as seen from
the hill above the house
through an opening in the wall
surrounding the outdoor stair.

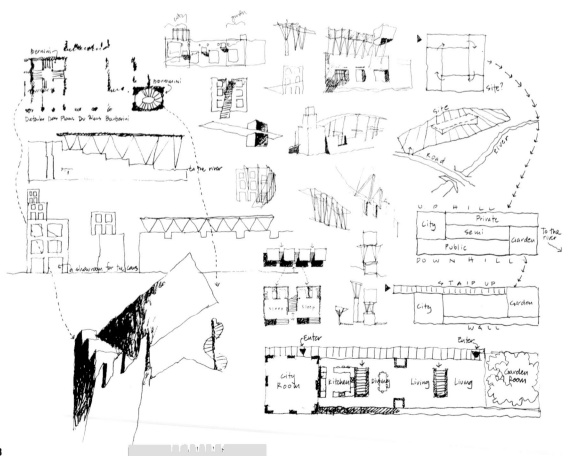

▲ *The street ends where the house begins.*

**DREAM HOUSE
the enigma of
the rooms**

from

The Architect's Dream:
Houses for the Next Millennium

sponsor

The Contemporary Arts Center
Cincinnati, Ohio

exhibited

1993

Curated by Daniel Friedman, the Dream House Exhibition invited ten architects to consider the house as not only a place, but as a landmark for how people think of themselves and their cities. In some cases the houses were sculptural, in others they embraced forms which could be considered iconographic. For us a house should reflect the uncertainty of the times; it should be enigmatic and vague.

Reflecting this objective all the lots in this city are vacant, and the rooms form streets crisscrossing the landscape and extending to the horizon. The plan is just one room after the other. The rooms do not form houses, which do not form blocks, which do not form neighborhoods. The hierarchy of the city is exchanged for a system of increasing entropy. The rooms define a fabric where the difference between one place and another becomes blurred and ambiguous.

The typical suburban house is centered on its lot, with most of the site as leftover space between the neighbors. In this dream, the land is spared, or at least excused. It is no longer the leftover, unseen space between inward-looking houses. Instead, the out-of-doors becomes a sanctuary, a place that is left alone, always having a presence in the surrounding "streets" of rooms.

Once the land and culture worked together to make every place different; one town was different from another. The people who lived in a town felt rooted to the community, where everyone was the same. This is the way it is remembered.

Modern people are rootless; their past is not shared with others. Here are rooms for individuals, but none for the community. ■

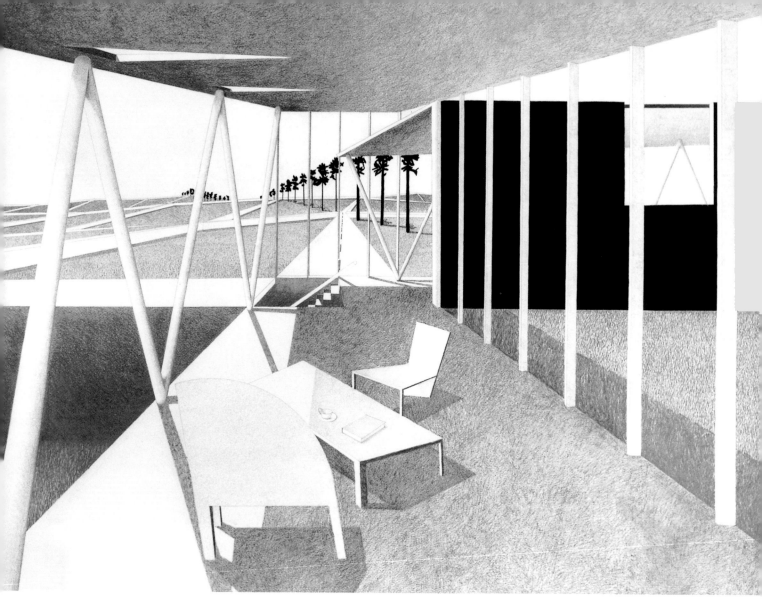

▲ From the living room, looking back toward the front door and the streets leading to the house.

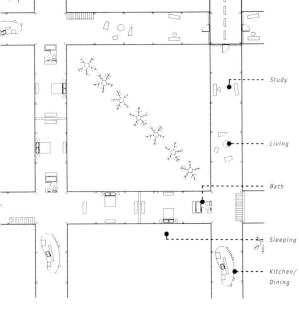

Study

Living

Bath

Sleeping

Kitchen/
Dining

▲ Floor plan with typical room icons noted.

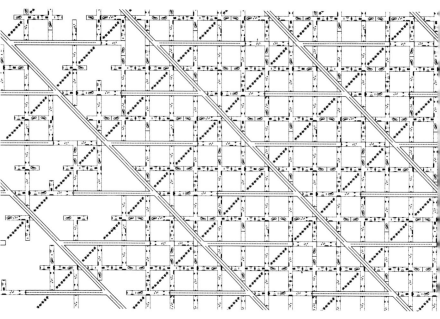

▲ The pattern of rooms and streets expands across the landscape.

PRESSURE

There is an artist called Cindy Sherman who has produced a series of photographs which she calls "Film Stills." The conceit behind this work is of isolated frames from a movie. Each shot is an evocative, costumed self-portrait in which Sherman dresses as some resonant female image in order to show the primacy of that image in inventing—not merely representing—women. Sherman appropriates a familiar cinematic context by placing herself in its midst. Importantly, in most of these "stills" her eyes are fixed on someone or something out of frame, imposing the idea of a missing narrative.[1]

MICHAEL SORKIN

▲ Film Still Untitled #137 *by Cindy Sherman, 1984. Courtesy the artist and Metro Pictures.*

Years pass, the myth evolves, Cindy Sherman reinvents herself in another photograph—*Untitled #137.* The pressure is written on her face. She sits alone; her hands are dirty. One interpretation makes her a symbol for all those people and things which have been transformed by the city's pressures. She is without a past, beyond the shelter of any community. Leaving has its risks. Failure is possible.

These pressures also transform architecture. The value of buildings has always been measured against the history already recorded in the architecture of a place. Once upon a time a place mattered because it was the foundation of all judgments and interpretations. Leaving home, the pressures of the city separate everyone from the history that made the past, present, and future of a single place important, whether it is a room, a building, a public space, or a neighborhood. Looking at

this picture of Cindy Sherman, what place matters to her?

Only when the context becomes dysfunctional is there a movement to rethink what has been accepted. Early attempts at the modernist city did not work in either Europe or the United States. Only in the U.S. has the failure of modernism been the catalyst for rejecting attempts to define an appropriately modern landscape. This is not surprising. In the U.S., experience has always been the accepted test. While the test of experience has inhibited the adoption of a modern style, the accompanying decline of the rule of tradition has just as effectively promoted undisciplined change.

In the past, change in architecture occurred in a disciplined and evolutionary way—the future evolved from the past. Old buildings became the precedent for future buildings; there was logic in this evolution. For instance, Auguste Perret's Notre Dame at Le Raincy in the 1920s drew on Gothic precedents in both the modulation of light with colored glass and the concrete vaulting. Perret was trying to be part of an older system; listening to precedent, he found logic for the evolution of his modern building. Since the precedent was an accepted part of the larger context, by implication this context would comfortably accept his new building.

Today, no one really looks to precedents anymore; they are used when convenient, and not to make a specific connection to the past. Precedents become something else entirely, for example, when a Gothic church is the precedent for a shopping mall. In this mode of thought, the architect is free to look to almost any precedent as the basis for almost any building, insuring that cities and towns will be composed of more and more exceptions. The context becomes a set of unrelated ideas that can be rethought in an instant. This condition is not new. In the nineteenth century in the U.S., fascination with stylistic experiments in home design saw classical, Gothic, Georgian, Italianate, and other styles lining the average street. These buildings foreshadowed twentieth-century experiments in the International Style, moderne, and other forms of modern expressionism. The styles of the nineteenth century, which invited experimentation, ironically became the bogeyman for "revolutionary" thinkers such as Wright and Bruce Goff. In America, architectural ideas both large and small compete.

Ultimately the context of the American city is a never-ending fabric of exceptions. Different visual ideas rub elbows along one street after another. Each building is comfortable in its own conception, but taken as a whole these exceptions weaken one another and fail to define a systematic tradition that can define what is appropriate. Without this measure the context lacks the means to affect the future.

When the fabric of buildings that makes up a city ceases to function as an anchor, then the context itself becomes less important and more pliable. Today almost anything can be considered the context. Wandering through Oklahoma, through Norman, Tulsa, and Bartlesville, quiet residential streets of very ordinary suburban homes are punctuated with some frequency by the houses of Bruce Goff. Not his major works, these are small, inexpensive, and completely outlandish works built for middle-class middle managers— ordinary people who accepted extraordinary ideas. Individual decisions replace the collective reflections of the community. In the U.S., whatever "is"—Goff's houses for example—becomes the context.

Individuals are comfortable with the American street that expresses an open-ended and plastic imagery. They are similarly drawn to buildings with imagery that is equally plastic. Early in this century hundreds of movie palaces were constructed. For a very few years, when the technology of film was relatively crude, these richly decorated and spatially complex buildings were highly successful in supporting the theater experience. Each building contained a clear narrative or plot line. The building and the film were tied together in creating an illusion and suspending the disbelief of the audience. But once the technology of film developed, these elaborate theaters were no longer needed. Difficult to adapt to new uses, only a few of them survive today. Yet the movie palace fit perfectly an old definition of architecture, where plan, form, and materials all support a single clear narrative.

Unlike the movie palace, most buildings in the U.S. maintain a narrative that is often unclear, unreadable, or missing—similar to Cindy Sherman's *Film Stills*. People devoted to systematic traditions find this condition disturbing. There are frantic attempts to regain the coherence of the imagined past. The result of this mania is often monotony—the minimalist imagery of downtowns dominated by Miesian office towers or the endless rows of picturesque houses in the suburbs.

This mania is blind to the unexpected meaning of the *Film Stills*. In a gallery with walls lined with images of Cindy Sherman, each image appears to be taken from a different movie. As a first impression each image is unrelated to the next, each is impaired by an incomplete narrative. But walking from one photograph to the next it finally becomes clear that the whole is undeniably powerful because Cindy Sherman is the exception which connects and dominates every image. Everybody can see themselves in each of these imagined films. At some time we have all stood on the hard pavement, suitcase in hand, wondering if we are going in the right direction.

Similarly, each of us can see ourselves in the Georgian or Victorian or modern houses lining a typical street. Each building is a different idea that is never fully understood. Each invites us to participate in completing the missing narrative, one reinforcing the other, just as one photograph reinforces the next on the walls of the gallery. In either case all of these unanswered questions define both a place and time without insisting on the systematic message expected in both photographs and buildings. Taken as a whole, the typical U.S. street accepts contradictions and anticipates the unexpected, the novel, and the outlandish. These visual forms of civil disobedience enhance the street.

In places rich in tradition, the meaning of a street or town could be destroyed by disobedient and unruly behavior. If a place is expected to offer answers, visual rules to live, then anything that fractures this context would be disturbing. In contrast, a street in the U.S. is far less fragile, offering everyone a place, avoiding answers, and leaving the completion of the narrative up to the imagination of the individual. This is comfort without community, relieving the pressure to find shared symbols and histories in a place where people share very little. ■

▲ *The reception area looking toward the front door.*

client
U.S.Robotics Corporation
site
Morton Grove, Illinois
completed
1994

Built in the 1950s, the manufacturing plant is a large, rectangular, single-story space of 250,000 square feet. The main office areas were programmed to run along the west and north edges of the rectangle from the northwest corner of the building. The entry and related functions define a north/south axis, anchored at the reception area. A much longer east/west axis is launched from this point, at the corner of the old building. This second axis leads to the main office areas, which run for 300 feet along one edge of the production floor. The up-and-down movement of the old shed roof is reflected in the hyperactive movement of panels of woven metal over the main corridor.

At its highest point, the interior clear height is only 14 feet above the floor. The interior horizon seems infinitely distant. The plan of the building is monumental, but any defining interior space to match its proportions is missing.

The horizontal extension of the space is never interrupted,

35

but the office space is compressed and then released by a series of large cylinders, known in the lexicon of the staff as "reactors." These objects contain the most sacred elements in the office, the copiers and coffee machines. The axial extension of space is never terminated. The question "Where are we going?" is never answered; the narrative is never complete.

The vast open space has been transformed, becoming a climate-controlled manufacturing space. The offices for the manufacturing group, running along the north edge of the larger space, obey the limitations of the building; no attempt is made to make vertical what is infinitely horizontal. Instead, the horizontal dimensions of the space are accepted and then exaggerated. A monumental interior space is found in the repetition of similar elements, over and over, until the very distant interior horizon is reached. ■

◄ *The path along a series of small conference rooms looking toward the front door.*

▲   *With one of the service areas in the foreground, the path back to*
      the reception area is marked with mesh ceiling panels.

◄   *The vertical strips of fluorescent light in the corridor are transposed*
      in the main conference room to lines of light in the ceiling.

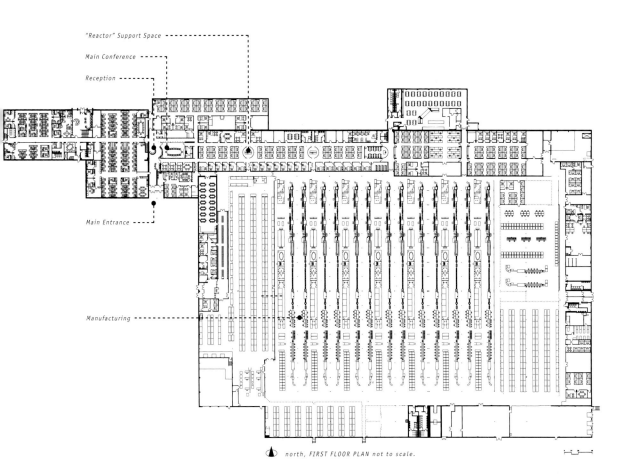

"Reactor" Support Space

Main Conference

Reception

Main Entrance

Manufacturing

north, FIRST FLOOR PLAN not to scale.

◄ The pattern of the roof is recalled in office partitions and mesh panels, only with a more frenzied frequency.

◄◄ Standing beside one of the service areas, nicknamed the "reactor" by the staff, the ceiling of the open office area follows the line of the pitched roof of the manufacturing plant.

NBC NEWS BROADCAST STUDIO

client
NBC News

site
Chicago, Illinois

completed
1996

The broadcast studio provided production facilities for NBC News during the 1996 Democratic National Convention at the United Center in Chicago. The entire facility was prefabricated and lowered into place as a single frame. Construction time was limited to five weeks, and the entire assembly was removed within a week after the convention was over.

The plan was composed of three spaces. The first and most important was the studio and the associated "porch," overlooking the convention floor. The second zone contained the support spaces behind the studio, which housed cameras and staff; and the third was the control room providing the station and the equipment for the director.

The image of the NBC studio at the 1996 Democratic National Convention reflects its expected role in this media event. Picture the United Center as an ocean of people—everyone trying to see or be seen. Over this ocean, cantilevered from an upper balcony, is a steel truss, the elliptical object standing in obvious contrast to the forms and materials of the stadium. The structure theatrically separates the people of NBC News from everyone else. The studio symbolizes the position of the fourth estate—the calm in the eye of the storm, a vantage point where perspective can be gained on the chaos below.

The people of the convention become the background of the set. Different camera positions give different perspectives on the convention. The NBC studio becomes the focus of everyone on the floor. It offers what everyone at the convention wants. It allows everyone to see (allies and competitors) and be seen (by allies and competitors). The message is never clear; implications are all that matter. ∎

▲   From above the steel skeleton of the studio is docked to the balcony of the United Center.

▲▲ The NBC News Studio appears as a target from the convention floor.

▲ *Across the bent and wrinkled form of the lawn, the south entry is centered on the line that divides the black grid from the white.*

SOUTH ENTRY FOR THE GRAND AVENUE

client
Milwaukee Redevelopment Corporation
site
Milwaukee, Wisconsin
designed
1984

Marshall Fields, the grand old Chicago department store, was supposed to build a new store as part of the "Grand Avenue," a retail center in downtown Milwaukee. Marshall Fields backed out, leaving a large hole along the back of the four-block-long development, which faces Michigan Avenue. The south entry fills this big, vacant space, providing energy where none seemed to exist.

Commissioned by the developer, Steve Dragos of the Milwaukee Redevelopment Corporation, the south entry is defined by three different fabrics rubbing up against one another. The first is a fabric of black lines on white covering the left half of the residual facade of the shopping mall—a wall that never expected to be seen. The other half of this face is covered with a similar fabric, but with the colors reversed. At the dividing line between these two grids is the doorway to the mall. The ground surface is painted with a third grid of concrete paths and grass. But in this case the surface is bent and warped by some unknown pressure channeling the pedestrians to the entrance. ∎

▲ From Delaware Street, Sinai Temple is divided into four quandrants by clerestory windows; the reception hall is to the left,the sanctuary to the right, and the religious school fills the two sections to the rear.

SINAI TEMPLE

designed jointly with
Searl and Associates, P.C.
client
Sinai Congregation
site
Chicago, Illinois
designed
1994

On a small urban lot in downtown Chicago, the programmed areas for a new temple were more than three times the site area, necessitating the consideration of a vertically layered building. This organization contradicts the more common single-level typologies of religious buildings. Most religions have an accepted building typology, usually reflecting the single building at the center of their world. Since the destruction of the Second Temple in Jerusalem, however, there has never been a sanctuary considered as the center of the Jewish world.

This absence diluted any attempts to define a single typology for synagogues. As a result a multilevel building could be used to solve the problems of a tight site. The reception hall, open to the street and sanctuary, occupies most of the first floor. The second floor houses the chapel and library, and the balconies of the sanctuary. The religious school and rooftop garden fill out the third floor.

This dense packing of functions is divided north/south and east/west by linear shafts bringing in daylight through clerestory windows. These light shafts appear as thick walls extending through the roof. Vaulted surfaces are compressed between these masses, each marking a ceremonial space. The largest vault spans the sanctuary. This space is entered from the reception hall; its arched ceiling acts as a buttressed vault to support the lawn of the roof garden just above the hall. On the uppermost floor, the focal point of the religious school is the gathering space. Its vaulted form is silhouetted against the skyline. On a more intimate scale, the curved roof surface of the second-floor chapel is an interior form which can be seen from the reception hall.

There is a code at work here—vaulted forms are compressed between walls by an implied stress from unknown origins. Each curved surface defines a sacred space: sanctuary, reception hall, chapel, and, finally, the gathering place for the school. Is there a new typology implied in the Sinai Temple? This is not likely. In the U.S., any building stands little chance of wide acceptance as a norm. There is just too little to connect. ■

third floor

second floor

first floor

lower level

north, *FLOOR PLANS* not to scale.

▶ The reception hall seen from the Delaware Street entry with light from the clerestory along the west and south edges.

▲ The sanctuary from the upper level of seats with light from the clerestory entering from above.

MAIN STORE
AND
ROOFTOP CAFE

client
Lincoln Park
Zoological Society
site
Lincoln Park Zoo in
Chicago, Illinois
projected completion
1999

The Lincoln Park Zoo began as a
single red brick building with a
hip roof and walls punctuated by
brick arches. This original building was completed in the neo-
prairie style common to most
nineteenth-century Chicago Park
District architecture. Upon the
zoo's expansion in the 1920s and

1930s other buildings were added
which seemed similar to the original structure, but there was a distinct shift toward neo-Georgian
designs. After the war, every style
was tried: buildings were buried
or built from poured-in or precast
concrete, old styles were revived,
and the history of architecture
was recalled. The practice of sim-
ulating nature in the exhibit habi-
tats, never a goal in the early
days of the zoo, became a mis-
sion, with tons of gunite used
to simulate rocks and trees. The
resulting campus provides a
precedent for almost any
approach.

Over the years the original
building was transformed. Built
into the side of a low rise in the

ground surface, the exposed
perimeter on three sides was covered in wire mesh and gunite.
With the removal of the hip roof,
the building disappeared entirely.
The single building, which should
be the precedent for everything
that followed, instead is remod-
eled to obey the "precedent" of
newer buildings.

The master plan for the zoo
calls for replacing this unrecog-
nizable building with a flight of
steps leading from the lower
southern portion of the zoo to
the higher northern portion. At
the center of the campus these
steps are wrapped around a new
two-level building. The lower level
houses the Zoological Society
store, while the upper level is a

belvedere used for cafe seating
and overlooking the outdoor
habitat for the lions.

The architecture of the steps
begins with the now missing original building. A 14-foot-high
brick wall is the starting point.
In plan the surface is bent into a
sine curve transforming the wall,
but maintaining a vague connection to the missing traditions. The
pattern in plan is extended to
define the form of the steps leading from the lower to the upper
level of the site. All this is topped
with a fabric canopy which forms
a wave pattern in elevation. The
red brick is expected, while the
curve is surprising, suggesting
something that is never fully
explained. ∎

ROOTLESS

When has a culture owed so little to its few "great" minds or its few hereditarily fortunate men and women? One of the contrasts between the culture of Europe and that of the United States is that the older culture traditionally depended on the monumental accomplishments of the few while the newer culture—diffused, elusive, process-oriented—depended on the novel, accreting ways of the many.[1]

DANIEL J. BOORSTIN

▲ Cathedrals of Space *by Roger Brown, 1983, lithograph/silk, is: 40x30 inches, ps: 46x36 inches. Courtesy of The Estate of Roger Brown and Phyllis Kind Gallery, New York.*

The space shuttle lifts off from the launching pad. The astronauts pilot the shuttle like a convertible with the top down. They thrill at the excitement of the liftoff. They wave happily to those left behind. The innocent emotion of the moment is captured in Roger Brown's *Cathedrals of Space.* The space shuttle is a silhouette, except for the glowing yellow windows where the astronauts wave to the earthbound crowds below. The pilots are not thinking of Plato pondering the universe. They are not thinking of Einstein theorizing about the organization of matter. They are not thinking about whether man's place is rightly at the center of the universe. Their thoughts are not rooted in any culture, but instead focus on the unknown future. They are experiencing the innocent thrill of rocketing off into space. They have left everything behind. They are only connected to the experience of the moment.

Today, earthbound Americans have much in common with the astronauts alone in space, preoccupied only with the moment. History, that inventory of common experiences, lessons, myths, and other bits of

memory, has been lost and replaced by the innocent thrill of the moment. The history of architecture, itself an inventory of commonly held images, both academic and vernacular, has suffered the same fate. Without history—without all those things that were once held in common—urban populations are rootless. Yet they can enjoy the innocent thrill of architecture.

To be modern means also to be rootless. "Community" is more and more broadly defined, embracing people who have less and less in common. Strangers compare notes on how many times they have moved, finding common ground in high numbers. What people have in common in the twentieth century is the understanding that they have so little in common. In this way people are bound to their century, if to nothing else. They understand they are no longer homogenous. Adolf Loos thought he saw the future in what he called the "migration of nations":

The speed of cultural evolution is reduced by stragglers. I perhaps am living in 1908, but my neighbor is living in 1900 and the man across

the way in 1880. It is unfortunate for a state
when the culture of its inhabitants is spread
over such a great period of time. . . . Happy
the land that has no such stragglers and
marauders. Happy America![2]

When Loos concluded, "The evolution of culture is synonymous with the removal of ornament from utilitarian objects,"[3] he saw architecture without ornament as appropriate for modern nations. He compared the complex narrative of a building's ornament to a rich meal. Loos advocated a leaner diet of boiled vegetables in its place, suggesting a much simpler narrative devoid of ornament. He sensed the crisis of culture evident in the stylistic experiments of turn-of-the-century Europe and thought minimalism offered a new prescription. By simplifying and reducing the complexity of the narrative, he thought a modern place could be defined which would be coherent and easily understood by this new community of modern people. It is evident that he expected the lack of a common culture and history would make America this first modern place.

Taking this simplification a giant step further, Mies van der Rohe sought to drive minimalism to a logical conclusion in which the many historic building typologies would be reduced to a single archetypal form defining a new universal space. In Chicago the black grid of the 860 and 880 Lake Shore Drive Apartments, built from 1949 to 1951, are the precedents for the similarly gridded office towers he built a few years later. Buildings would be reduced to the most minimal elements; one form would work for any use. Not surprisingly, modern people accept the same form for both the home and the office. On any residential street it is clear that almost any form can be accepted as a house in America.

Unfortunately, few people found any thrill in the minimalism of universal space, or by comparison any delight in Loos's diet of boiled vegetables. The reduction underlying the logic of the grid implied very little. The possibility of the unexpected was reduced. Mies's argument missed the underlying complexity of the times. Modern people had already demonstrated a willingness to consider any form as appropriate for any use. Simplicity was not necessarily a part of the prescription. In the end, cool logic was not enough to compensate for the lack of any heated contradictions. There was greater comfort in complex buildings that cannot be fully understood, suggesting that missing narrative. Instead of accepting one form that would work for any use, in the U.S. any form would work for any use.

The Virginia state capitol bears a striking resemblance to the porticos of the 1970s-vintage Ramada Inn. After Jefferson's capitol was complete, and with little notice, Greek revival buildings became a "new tradition" for all types of government buildings. Similarly, but with some help from paid advertising, the Greek portico became a "new tradition" symbolizing a motel chain to the U.S. traveler. Did Jefferson and the anonymous architect of these motels expect the same traditional form to have the same meaning? It is more likely that they both expected the meaning of the form could be rewritten at will.

Jefferson reused, and at times transformed, the precedents he knew from his studies and travels to respond to his own sense of an appropriate architecture. He understood the origins of these forms. He most likely did not expect his audience to have a similar understanding. In a letter to James Madison he wrote:

> I have received an application from the Directors of the public buildings, to procure them a plan for their capitol. I shall send them one taken from the best morsel of ancient architecture now remaining.. It has obtained the approbation of fifteen or sixteen centuries, and is therefore, preferable to any design which might be newly contrived. It will give more room, be more convenient, and cost less, than the plan they sent me. Pray encourage them to wait for it, and to execute it. It will be superior in beauty to any thing in the world. It is very simple.[4]

His use of the Maison Carrée in Nîmes for the new capitol was convenient. He could describe the solution as simple even though the building was based on a highly complex ornamental system. The tone of his letter to Madison indicates he suspected the design would not be fully understood. If anything, he considered his use of precedent as part of a lesson painted large across the landscape. This is certainly the case with the ten pavilions at the University of Virginia—each a lesson in the proper proportioning of a classical facade.

His use of these images was studied, practical, and convenient. He thought that in his modern America of two hundred years ago, old forms would be accepted as a new norm based on new readings. Like Loos he sought a new prescription. Indeed, his architecture would be accepted, but not as a new normative image. Instead, the architecture he popularized would compete with other ideas, reused and redefined over and over again until Jefferson's favorite forms lost their intended meaning. There is nothing wrong with the Virginia capitol and the Ramada Inn sharing the use of a classical portico. The use of the form is convenient in both cases. Each is appropriate because the temple form has lost its meaning, not because it ever had any.

In the U.S. almost any image becomes a blank slate on which almost anything can be written. The Ramada Inn took advantage of this condition to write its own highly commercial message in the blank space. But only through the repeated reinforcement of advertising is it possible to sustain the narrative that connects form and message. It is evident that the U.S. is a modern place. Places where history loses its importance are all modern. ■

▲ The entire box is made of 3/16-inch aluminum plate including the stair cantilevered from the wall. The panels on the right swing open, giving someone in the bath a view of Lake Michigan.

◄ From the front door, two wood walls shape the space, focusing on the John Hancock Center in the distance.

▼ Axonometric of the metal and wood boxes defining the volumes of the ceremonial spaces and beyond their walls, a floor plan of the service areas.

GARDNER APARTMENT

designed jointly with
Michael Cygan
client
Tracy Gardner
site
Chicago, Illinois
completed
1994

In America, from the very earliest period, the methods of construction have undergone important and symbolic transformations. The substance of traditional buildings has been replaced with an architecture of increasing thinness; everything substantial becomes lighter, at times almost weightless. Thin stud walls of wood and plywood have replaced thick walls of stone and masonry. The Gardner apartment extends this trend to its ultimate conclusion.

The "site" is less than 1,200 square feet on the fifty-eighth and fifty-ninth floor of a Michigan Avenue high-rise. The apartment's view is dominated by the dark looming mass of the John Hancock Center to the north. The apartment is divided between "ceremonial" and functional spaces. Within the empty volume defined by the perimeter walls of the apartment, two idealized boxes are inserted: one of metal on the first floor, and the other of wood on the second. Each box is impossibly thin, containing just barely enough substance to retain its form. The choice of materials is not based on their individual characteristics; instead they are chosen because they are different from one another, and from the surrounding drywall box of the apartment building. These containers enclose the ceremonial space within the apartment.

In homage to the John Hancock Center, each box is warped by the tower's imagined gravitational pull. The aluminum shell, defined by a series of straight lines, is either orthogonal to the city grid, or to the angled sides of the tower. The curves of the wood shell are tangential to an imagined circle passing through the four outer corners of the Hancock.

The leftover space between these new containers and the apartment walls provides the bare minimum of space required for the "messy" functions of cooking, bathing, and storage. Almost every surface of each container is hinged, providing access to the different functional areas. The stair connecting the upper and lower ceremonial spaces is so thin it defies explanation.

The tendency to reduce materials to their most minimal state reminds us of our rootlessness. Sheet metal becomes thinner, trusses more ephemeral, gypsum board is substituted for plaster, plastic replaces everything else, and, finally, dialogue is replaced by the monologue of voice mail. The process of reduction and substitution, begun three centuries ago, has reached its ultimate and absurd conclusion in the impossible thinness of the Gardner Apartment. ■

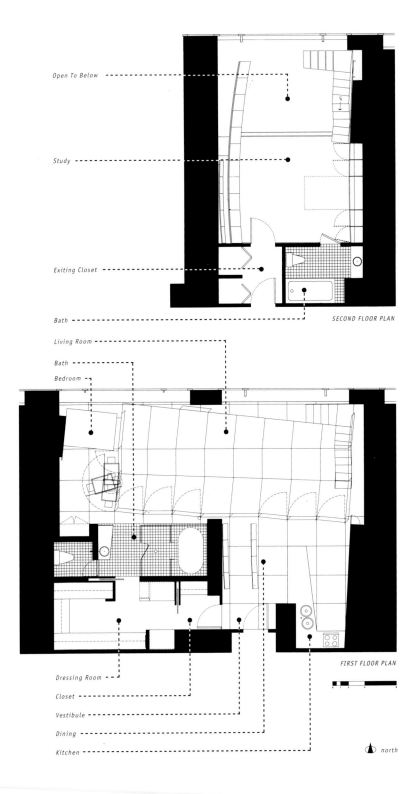

Open To Below

Study

Exiting Closet

Bath

SECOND FLOOR PLAN

Living Room

Bath

Bedroom

FIRST FLOOR PLAN

Dressing Room

Closet

Vestibule

Dining

Kitchen

north

▲ Falling is the dominant thought as the impossibly thin surface of the stair leads toward the window and the street far below.

► The media equipment is stacked vertically on a revolving panel which at one moment is part of the ceremonial living space and at the next moment is part of the sleeping area.

►► From the bathroom the bed can be seen past the revolving media center on the right.

▼ Impossibly thin walls separate the ceremonial spaces from the messy zones for bathing, eating, storage, and sleeping. In this case the aluminum panels of the living space have been swung open so the lake can be seen through the glass walls of the shower.

▲ *Three aluminum planes swing open to connect the living space to the kitchen.*

▲ The one-thousand-foot-long east facade is punctuated at four points by cylindrical spaces leading to the interior courtyards.

◄ Two blocks of apartments and the curved form of the mechanical plant define the entry to one of the courtyards.

ARBOUR PARK APARTMENTS

client

Arbour Development Company

site

Tempe, Arizona

completed

1985

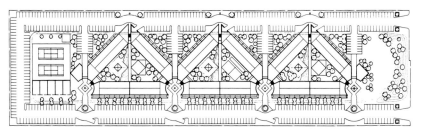

➤ north, SITE PLAN not to scale.

Along this stretch of Apache Boulevard in Tempe, Arizona, there is a bowling alley, a motorcycle repair shop, small factories, places to eat, a car wash, a lot covered with abandoned school buses. The larger neighborhood has many places to work but few places to live. Arbour Park Apartments revisits the notion of worker housing, transplanting European housing concepts to the Sunbelt: affordable housing for the working class with one distinction—this project was not subsidized by any company or government. Success would be determined on the open market.

Richard Marmor, the developer, believed that to be successful, the project had to be "sold" to prospective tenants, who included some students, some lower-level white-collar workers, but mostly blue-collar workers. These tenants selected Arbour Park from a marketplace which includes any number of low-cost rental apartments. For this reason, the project had to be both low in cost and extraordinary in design.

A budget of $26,000 per unit included land cost, all site improvements, and furniture in each of the 278 units. The materials used in its construction—

▲ *The forced perspective of the west elevation.*

▼ *The requisite pool, symbol of the southwest.*

concrete block walls, wood framing, a stucco veneer—are part of a U.S. tradition of cheap, fast construction. Add other equally common materials—concrete roofing tiles, aluminum slider windows, and rough-sawn lumber—and this project might be indistinguishable from any number of ordinary buildings stretching across the United States.

Yet Arbour Park is different. Its design proposes to make the ordinary monumental, so that from whatever angle, whatever approach, the buildings are exaggerated, made larger, bigger. Size creates significance. Space is compressed between elements of great mass. The outdoor spaces seem to have been cut from a single mass of masonry.

Once inside the courtyards, scale and distances are reduced. The swimming pool and barbecue pavilion are symbols of leisure. These are places to meet your temporary neighbors, talk about the Phoenix Suns, have a beer. The courtyards are outdoor living rooms, made even more important by the small size of the apartments.

In achieving the tension between space and object, precedents were used when convenient. The plasticity of Piazza San Ignazio, the transparency of layered openings arranged along an axis, and allusions to infinite baroque facades are all at play in this project. These precedents were useful, but their traditional meanings are no longer important. Each tenant's place of origin is different, each tenant sees in a different language. They share this place for a short period of time, before continuing their journeys. The transient population of Arbour Park is just a small cross section of the nation's rootless population. ■

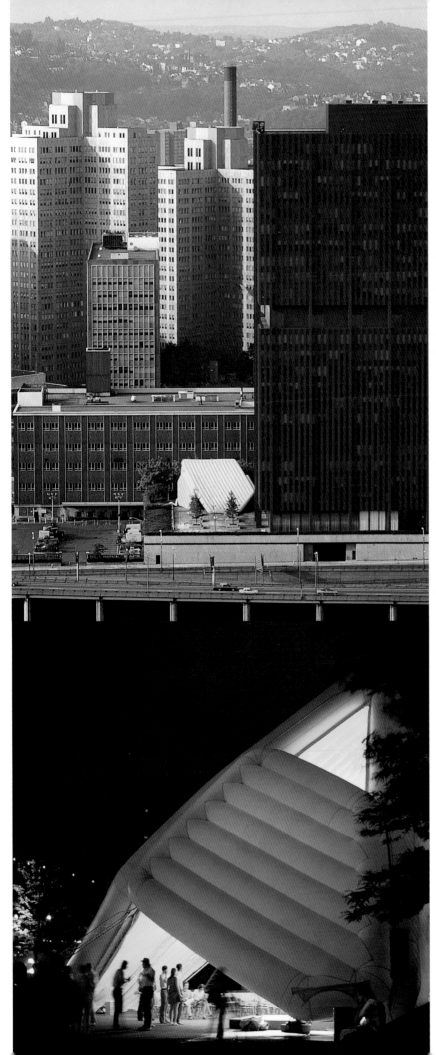

THREE RIVERS EVENTSTRUCTURE

designed jointly with
Kent Hubbell
client
The Carnegie Art Institute
Pittsburgh, Pennsylvania
completed
1975

A woman of some years passes by and asks if we have seen the "life raft?" Can we direct her there? She comments that all her friends are talking about it after seeing it in the Sunday newspaper. Suddenly, all those intentions that once were so important are lost. This building was supposed to be all about implied mass. The structure that in truth weighs less than a pound per square foot has a presence implying a far greater weight—air made visible and solid at the same time.

Erected once a year, the building provided a performance space during the annual summer art festival in Pittsburgh sponsored by the Carnegie Art Institute. Just over 2,000 square feet in area, the structure seated two hundred people. It could be erected in a few days on the plaza of the Westinghouse Building.

As Joan Ockman suggests in "Pneumotopian Visions" in *Metropolis*, " . . . the blow-up structure was seen as an anti-

monumental—and therefore anti-establishment—answer to the avant-garde's desire for emancipation through technology. Fluidly indeterminate, user oriented, sensuous, and mobile, it seemed responsive to a dawning eco-consciousness on the part of consumers who demanded instant gratification and throwaway expendability."[5] This is only one interpretation. Despite the image of these soft buildings, the values of the new technology was questioned by people on the far left who saw any building as an expression of the "dominant power system."

Now, the gray-haired woman raises her own questions, providing her own narrative. Intentions mean nothing. Instead she has superimposed her own interpretation. Her unexpected insights suggest that the experience measures up to her expectations. None the less, her interpretation, based on her own experience, reinforces the ambiguity of the structure. ∎

▲ *The city of Pittsburgh, grey and anonymous, is punctuated by the Eventstructure on the Westinghouse Plaza.*

◄ *At night the solidity of the form loses its mass as light dematerializes the form.*

... though present throughout the hemisphere that restlessness and all it entails have been most intensely experienced in . . . the United States. Its people have always been the most adrift from precedent; their culture has consistently remained that of a frontier—at first a physical, later a social and technological one. The cataclysmic modern shift from the small, pre-industrial world to a new world of mass population and industrialism did not begin in America, but when it came to these shores it developed faster and more completely in the United States than anywhere else in the world. This must have taken place partly because there was less of the old in America to hold off the new and partly because of the character of the American himself. The rush of immigration which began in the 1840s exacerbated an archetypal colonial sense of uprootedness and partial alienation and it eventually swept away that anchor in classical learning and in the cult of intellectual attainment which has been the true distinction of, and, indeed, the spur to, reasoned revolutionary action in late colonial and early republican society. So the American became the first mass man, the first modern man, trampling over the earth and all old things. It is no wonder that the first characteristic forms of twentieth-century architecture began to take shape in his hands.[1]

VINCENT SCULLY

▲ Assassination Crucifix by Roger Brown, 1975, oil/canvas, 70x96 inches. Courtesy of The Estate of Roger Brown and Phyllis Kind Gallery, New York.

The average American willingly embraces progress, while at the same time worshiping all things from the past. The past, made up of memories of a connected set of values and histories, is often represented by a building, a public square, a street, or some other place. Preserving the past often means resisting progress. Embracing progress means accepting the costs of change "and trampling over the earth and all old things."

Remnants of the past are everywhere in the United States. History is an obsession. Everything imaginable is recorded and stored in photographs, files, and electronic media. Americans understand that in other countries buildings are the ever-present visual records of the past. There is a rush to preserve older buildings and historic districts, and to build new places similar to these "originals" with the same look and feel. History still offers lessons, but it no longer plays the same active role in making judgments; it has become only something to be preserved.

The past is safe; an idealized vision people carry around as baggage, in which things were slower, more certain, properly constrained, more comfortable, and less threatening. The bags are packed and people are ready to leave for this remembered past but unfortunately everyone has a different destination. People have their own private history, places that matter, ethnic histories they were taught, their own leaders. People in the same neighborhood do not share the same memories. Events have been recorded, but everyone remembers a different history.

A building is preserved to maintain the continuity of history. Yet every neighborhood is in a constant state of flux. People move in and others move out. The historic continuity of a place is of limited value if it is not shared by everyone. The past does not represent a working set of images and values used by people to judge and interpret change. Instead the past becomes idealized, vague, and slippery. History is only a measure of the social, technical, and emotional distance that people have traveled, a measure of how far we have progressed.

In most other countries the competition between the resistance of history and the pressures of progress is less contradictory; the dominant culture remains dominant, making the population much more homogeneous. People remember the same history; the common memories offer comfort from the uncertainty of change. Both the new and the old are judged in the same context. Exceptions occur when new immigrants replace once-dominant people and a homogeneous culture is imported. The U.S. is the exception to such exceptions.

For all of those migrating to this shore the physical places that once supported their ethnic memories are now distant. Over time memories are lost and nothing takes their place. This separation ripples through everything that is seen, touched, and heard, undermining the inertia of history that once dampened the speed of change. Lacking this restraint, contradictions multiply, the ties binding the past, present, and future together are loosened. This irreversible separation from the past is a necessary condition for modernization. Because it happened here first, America is the first modern place.

Usually both the catalyst and the symbol for modernization is the city—a place where one is separated from one's roots, where the ties binding an older culture together are loosened, and where new places allow the acceptance of new ways. In most places, urbanization occurs gradually, but in the U.S. migration to a new continent ignited the process of dislocation, and the accompanying urbanization compounded this separation. While moving was once unusual, it has become expected. People now move from region to region, from country to city, from city to suburb, from suburb back to the country. With little thought one place is abandoned for another. Modernization is taken to the extreme. America is the relentlessly modern nation.

This restlessness redefines architecture. Whereas buildings were once memorable for the thoughts they symbolized, now they are expected to create memories. This change is illustrated in the changing role of the "landmark." Once a landmark was a visual icon that represented a very specific set of memories of the surrounding city. Now landmarks have been reduced to a measure of time and distance. They indicate nothing more than departure or arrival, sometimes measured at the speed of the pedestrian, while in other cases they are measured at the speed of the car. In Chicago, the Sears Tower marks the city as a destination. But what is Chicago? It is not a specific place; it is a confusion of different and contradictory thoughts similar to other U.S. cities. Landmarks no longer serve to slow change, they only serve to measure the rate of change. The architecture of the Sears Tower is memorable, but the memories it symbolizes are fuzzy and vague.

Symbolic of the decreasing inertia of history is the effort to make people comfortable with uncertainty by packaging change as a "new tradition." This tag line, suggesting a new norm, raises the question of whether the past has been studied to discover as yet undiscovered lessons or has simply been replaced. The lack of any widespread surprise over these "new traditions" implies people's never-ending willingness to consider the new and novel. In America, the experience of the moment is much more important than the memory of the past. This is true for anything, from the daily menu to vacation destinations. If it is convenient and of apparent value, the term "new traditions" can be used to make change acceptable.

For the most part, Americans will not accept normative thinking, whether for new traditions or older ones. With very little history held in common, few things are understood in the same way. For this reason searching for new norms of thought is an impossible task; normative and modern are mutually exclusive terms.

The absence of a shared history makes the acceptance of any new language impossible, in spite of its logic. When people began coming apart instead of coming together is difficult to document, but the absence of a shared history was noticed in Roger Brown's *Assassination Crucifix*. The street intersection in Dealey Plaza is seen from above; each of the street corners is projected into the third dimension using a different axis. The form of a crucifix appears, implying an ending and a beginning.

At this moment in Dallas, people understood that something had come to an end. The narrative of history had been interrupted. A new understanding of the past would be needed to explain the present. The formulation of this understanding is still missing. Looking farther back, this interdependence has been missing for a long time; 1963 marks the date when people took notice. Without this shared understanding connections between intent and form will be uncertain.

People write their own narratives, reaching their own conclusions, making the understanding of all buildings innocent and, in a way, naive. It is like listening to directions in a foreign tongue. Something is being said, yet there seems to be an infinite number of ways to interpret the instructions. The architecture of every building, new or old, is written in a different and foreign tongue. Interpretations multiply, making the meaning of every building and every place ambiguous. Modern places can be identified by an inability to specify or prescribe how buildings will be interpreted. This happens in places where people are rootless. For "the first mass man," "the first modern man," history is over, no longer providing the foundation for normative thinking or for a common understanding of architecture.

In America the memories of the past are weakened and are never fully formed. The past is worshipped, but this motive is always subordinated to the embrace of progress. ■

▲ *The overlapping roofs define different functional spaces including the deli with its glass window overlooking the parking lot.*

BEANS AND BARLEY MARKET AND CAFE

client
2B REAL LLC

site
Milwaukee, Wisconsin

completed
1994

The owners of Beans and Barley are all successful survivors of the sixties. The business started in 1971, growing to over one hundred employees. With an emphasis on vegetarian and organic preparations, the market and cafe were a success anticipating the trend to offer foods and beverages in a number of different ways under a single roof: a bar, a restaurant, a grocery, and a deli are all housed in the same 10,000-square-foot space. Just when they thought they knew what to expect, the restaurant burned to the ground—or at least to the top of the old foundation.

Built on the foundation of the old building, on a triangular lot with acute angles, in the midst of a dense urban area, the new design metabolizes the original patterns of structure, defining a new form. From Kenilworth, the quieter side street, the building rises until the roof shapes seem to dissipate their energy against the edge of North Avenue, the main commercial street of the area. Below these roof surfaces a two-story dining room announces the arrival of vegetarian culture on Milwaukee's East Side.

The components of the building are decidedly metabolic—the repeated "V" shapes are whisks, the brick is eggplant, the paint is avocado in color—until steel and masonry become almost digestible. The forms all have some analogy to food. These connections explain only the origin of the respective forms; they do not define a narrative. The metabolic ornament is only further evidence that any precedent can be used for any building. ■

▶ Along North Avenue the curved roofs of the restaurant, screen over the nightclub stair and canopy over the front door dominate the horizon.

▶▶ The canopy over the entrance frames older retail buildings across North Avenue.

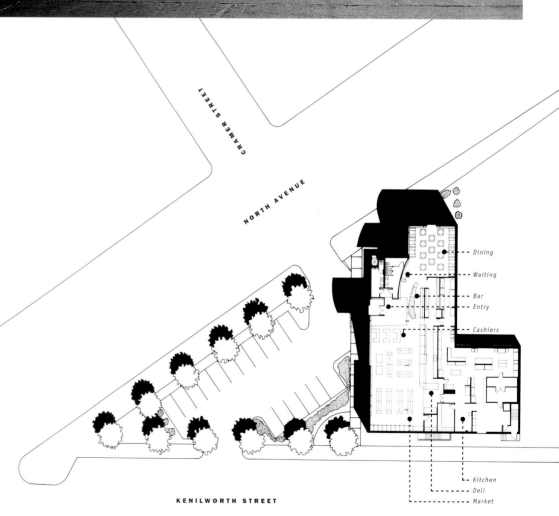

CRAMER STREET

NORTH AVENUE

OAKLAND AVENUE

OAKLAND AVENUE

— Dining

— Waiting

— Bar

— Entry

— Cashiers

KENILWORTH STREET

— Kitchen
— Deli
— Market

NORTH, site plan not to scale.

PLAINFIELD TOWN CENTER DESIGN COMPETITION

site
Plainfield, Illinois
designed
1997

What the modern community searches for in the face of postmodern disorder is comfort. The obvious response is history—comfort drawn from everything which is familiar and common. The front porch, the little shop, the traditional lamp post—anything from the past seems an appropriate response to the ambiguity and complexity of the times. There is a logic to this search. In the face of a dysfunctional present, building the things that work from the past makes sense. But, at heart, this search is for comfort and not for history.

Following a different path in this search, the plan for Plainfield embraces postmodern disorder, finding in its most prevalent icons a future that is open, green, and offers a place for all the events and experiences which define the U.S.—a comfortable place where the bonds to the past have been loosened and new ways can be accepted. The primary determinant of the town center is the car. This city can be seen fast. Yet the movement of cars is efficiently managed in the grid of streets, preserving the majority of the town center for green space. When filled, the surface lots are planned to make each car contribute to a sculptural pattern.

▲ *View of the Plainfield City Hall overlooking the park to the west.*

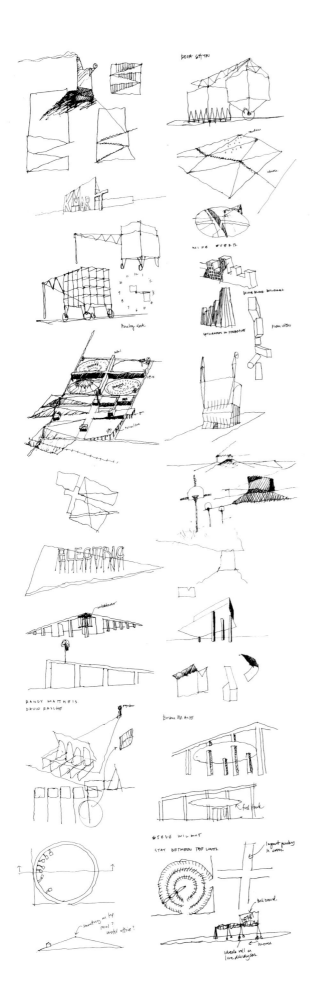

▲ The sweep of the park is interrupted by three curious and unexplained basketball hoops.

▲▲ A rest area near the commercial-retail center.

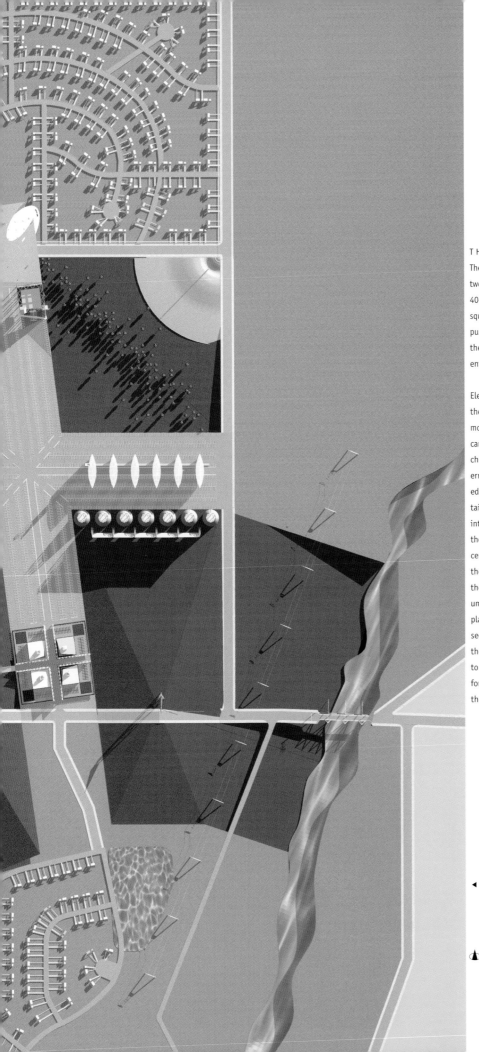

THE PLAN

The entire plan is divided into two major areas, each a square 40-acre parcel of land. The square to the east is devoted to public enterprise. To the west, the square is devoted to private enterprise.

After crossing the bridge and Electric Park from the old town, the first parcel is used for common activities from cradle (daycare) to grave (-yard), from church to state (municipal government), and from rethinking education to reinventing entertainment. The parcel is divided into four square quarters with the tower of the town hall at the center. Facing north, the area to the left of the hall is all about the past—the school, the museum, and the cemetery are here, places where history can be seen and learned. To the right of the town hall the functions look to the future. The park is a platform of land under which are the police and fire facilities; just to the south is the outdoor movie screen of the movie palace, and laundromat/computing center.

The second 40-acre parcel is a place for individual enterprise. Bisecting this square in one direction are the big-box retail stores, and bisecting the square in the other direction is the commercial center with offices and small scale retail. Each of these zones is served by great circles of parking, making a visual ballet out of finding an empty space. Anchoring the corners of this square are the four most important roadside experiences: take-out food, the car wash, the drugstore, and the donut shop. ■

◀ *Village center plan covering two quarter sections. The section to the left is planned for commercial, while the section to the right is planned for city and educational uses.*

◖ *north, SITE PLAN not to scale.*

COMMUNITY BUILDINGS

▶ *MOVIE PALACE*
The traditional movie palace is a place where every element, from the media to the environment, supports the suspension of disbelief. The Plainfield Movie Palace embraces this tradition, but abandons the old technology of film and projector in favor of new media dependent on digital technology.

▶ *INFO CENTER / LAUNDROMAT*
Traditionally, the Laundromat is a place to meet and talk with your neighbor. Its bulletin board, with messages about lost dogs and new roommates, remains an important service. In a town where everyone has a washing machine, there is still a need for a place where these interpersonal exchanges can occur. The Laundromat has undergone a transformation similar to the Movie Palace. The technology has changed, but the underlying importance remains the same.

▶ *SCHOOL (OF HISTORY)*
A school is first and foremost a place to learn the accepted history of things. When first-graders learn to add and subtract, they are learning the history of math. When high school students study the speed at which an object is accelerated by earth's gravity, they are learning the history of physics. The Plainfield school is a center for history, where students, from preschoolers up to the elderly, come to learn from the past.

▶ *POLICE / FIRE STATION*
An undulating roof covers the Police and Fire Station and provides the structure for an elevated park above.

◀ ELECTRIC PARK
The gateway to the Civic Center, Electric Park suggests a digital future. The bridge, crossing the Du Page River and connecting the old town and the new town, like the future, is purposely indeterminate.

◀ TOWN HALL
The two functions of the town hall—meeting hall and public offices—are intentionally separate. Elevated above the great lot, the container for the meeting hall dominates the public space. In turn, the public offices are under the wrinkled pavement that is warped and bent to form the front facade of the building. These offices overlook the covered court of the town hall and the adjacent park land.

◀ PLAINFIELD TOWN GREEN
One quarter section is committed to a town green. This section is then quartered by the great village parking lot into four park areas. Each park has a major public use.

COMMERCIAL BUILDINGS

◀ SUPERSTORE RETAIL CENTER
Category killers, big boxes. This is the flip side of the small specialty retail store, where all decisions are quantitative.

◀ COMMERCIAL CENTER
This is the office center for the entire community. The base of each building works together to form a retail arcade. The buildings appear to move, light and agile, in contrast to the earthbound mass of the big-box retail buildings.

◀ GAS STATION
The little secret of the town, figuratively located under the great plaza, is the place everyone must visit—the Plainfield gas station. In a world of LUST (Leaking Underground Storage Tanks), the gas station's design does not bury anything, the storage tanks are located overhead, suspended from the superstructure that supports the town square.

◀ MOTEL
Central to a sense of community is the act of making a visitor welcome. Too often, the values of some national hotel chain dominate, as opposed to local community values. In concept, each room in the Plainfield Motel is a house, a home, in fact, with its own sense of place, its own view of the surrounding community. Built on a hill, the motel complex follows a path, which begins at the roadside reception hall and ends at the hilltop pool.

◀ RANDY'S DONUTS
Threatened with demolition in a widening of Manchester Boulevard in Los Angeles, Randy's Donuts was saved by a corporate sponsor and moved to Plainfield. It is both the oldest building in the new town center and a monument to the great roadside architecture of the past.

▲ The long slender addition to the building curves to the left with the roofs of the entry and main banking room in the distance. The random corbelling of the brick is interrupted by stone panels recalling the iconography of the "Great Seal" on the back of the one dollar bill.

▼ The curved wall is broken at one point by the entry and main banking hall.

TEACHERS FEDERATION CREDIT UNION

client
Teachers Federation
Credit Union

site
Minneapolis, Minnesota

completed
1985

The great seal of the U.S. dollar is a pyramid with a glowing enigmatic eye at the pinnacle. People look at this icon every day and rarely question its presence on the most common of all currencies. It is an image of unknown origins and meaning which has been widely accepted.

Teachers Federation Credit Union is a small financial institution near Minneapolis, Minnesota. The original building was a hodge-podge of additions built over twenty years, with no front and no rear, meandering over a suburban site. The only recognizable form was a wedge-shape plan of the exterior walls generated by the triangular site.

In the renovation, these angled walls are accepted and in-filled in places to complete the form. The point where two walls would intersect in the distance becomes the center of an arc, which defines the outer limits of a new addition, with a curved facade forming the front of the building. The addition matches the height of the original building, except where the surface is broken by two aluminum-clad roofs defining the entry and main banking room.

Across this horizontal mass, a linear window dematerializes the wall. Then the great seal of the U.S. dollar is imposed as a series of triangular stone forms, the eye replaced by a rusticated stone panel at the pinnacle. The bankers considered the design, deemed it properly rooted in the history of a symbol they recognized but probably did not understand, and pronounced it buildable. ■

VIRTUAL COMFORT CHAIR

Introducing
the Fat or Non-fat
Christ or the Anti-Christ
Comfort or Virtual Comfort
Chair for a
Knoll Furniture Competition
designed
1996

Knoll International invited a group of Chicago architects to reinterpret their SoHo chair. Each designer rethought the concept of an office task chair, presenting their own prototype. This assignment seemed part of an increasingly common mode of thought—a single name, such as Thousand Island Dressing, used to describe different products whose qualities may differ or may be contradictory. Is it fat or non-fat? Is it a SoHo chair or not?

With a century of progress in ergonomic office design about to come to an end, there is the realization that the office is undergoing redefinition. Once the office was, more than anything else, a chair. The office was a place where workers could consider they had roots. The definition of an office is now ambiguous: is it an environment? Is it a means of communication? Is it a state of mind? Does it have anything to do with furniture? Now we are rootless, disconnected; the office has more to do with the imagination than a sense of place. The chair has been redefined to reflect this ambiguity. Is it a place to sit, or a symbol of change? Is comfort real or imagined? It embraces the ambiguity of the times. ■

INNOCENCE   COMFORT   SELF-EVIDENCE   AMBIGUITY

looking forward

Architecture is both intentional and accidental. The intentions reflect our opinions
about modern architecture in the late twentieth century. The accidents are unexpected
and unpredictable, and in turn transform our
opinions. These opinions and afterthoughts
are noted in the next four chapters—
INNOCENCE, COMFORT: A GUILTY PLEASURE,
SELF-EVIDENCE, and AMBIGUITY OF THE
MISSING NARRATIVE.

person becomes hesitant when a book, a movie, or a place to vacation becomes "too" popular. Offered the safety and shelter of new norms of thought, this refuge is rarely embraced by anyone. Just about everyone resists being indentured to hand-me-down thoughts. The persistence of our innocence lets us neglect the lessons of the present with the optimism that this is not as good as it gets. The next building is more interesting than the last one. Innocence values innovation over any established order. Choosing innovation is an act of civil disobedience—a willingness to try anything and then live with the consequences.

In the U.S., these acts of disobedience are encouraged by our absent memory of history, affording a perfect, naive freedom for both the makers of buildings and the users of buildings. This absence sustains innocence, allowing designers to innovate, abandoning the past and preconceived notions. Similarly, this absence limits people's expectations, which are fuzzy and vague.

The past can and often is embraced when innovation does not seem to be leading anywhere. It is embraced not because it is a part of history, but because it works. This results in the curious mix of invention and repetition in buildings. The established style may be accepted, but not because it is established. It is accepted only until some new innovation can overtake its established value. Ultimately, innocence expects innovation, and innovation is the antithesis of order.

Somehow these expectations are captured in Anselm Keifer's painting *Notung*. At first reading we see the grainy texture of a woodcut. Then out of the pattern a room appears of wooden floors, walls, and ceiling. Looking more closely, the primitive one-point perspective is disturbed by an iron sword stuck in the floor—a third reading holding a warning is discovered. Different layers are found in a single painting; each layer is innocent, easily understood, and each is a different thought.

Similarly, when buildings are composed of many different layers, each a different, easily digestible visual bite of data, the architecture reflects our innocence. People respond less to memories than to the thrill of discovering ideas—the more the better. Robert Venturi's simple sheds are built up from elemental forms, becoming complex assemblies of very different thoughts. In his words, these sheds accept the complex and contradictory and reject the single simple big idea as the ideal of late modernism. The ornament is traditional, but its application denies tradition. The sum of these very different thoughts, each simple and easily understood, is complex and contradictory.

We think a building should be composed of archetypal forms, simple geometries, grids, big forms capturing complicated programs, overscaled objects, and many other "big ideas." The more layers of thought, the more understandable each idea, the greater the sense of discovery.

Assembling a stream of different, yet easily digestible thoughts and ideas in a single building recognizes the innocence of pilgrims. Such an approach recognizes that each of us has some connection to those characters played by Jimmy Stewart; they are always optimistic, innocent, and on the move. ■

▲ A grove of pine trees separates the paper mill from the Health Center seen in the distance.

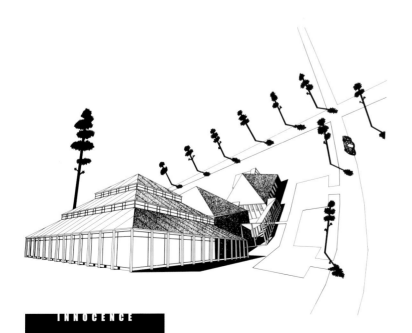

COOSA PINES HEALTH CENTER

client
Kimberly-Clark Corporation
site
Coosa Pines, Alabama
completed
1990

The site is at the edge of a major pulp and paper mill: smokestacks, debarking machines, noise—a relentless environment built for machines. The mill consumes trees and at the same time is surrounded by the dense forests of central Alabama. The 30,000-square-foot health center is located near the mill, within the forest.

The "building" is divided into four squares arranged in a row. Each square defines one of the four major program areas. Each is interpreted and developed differ-

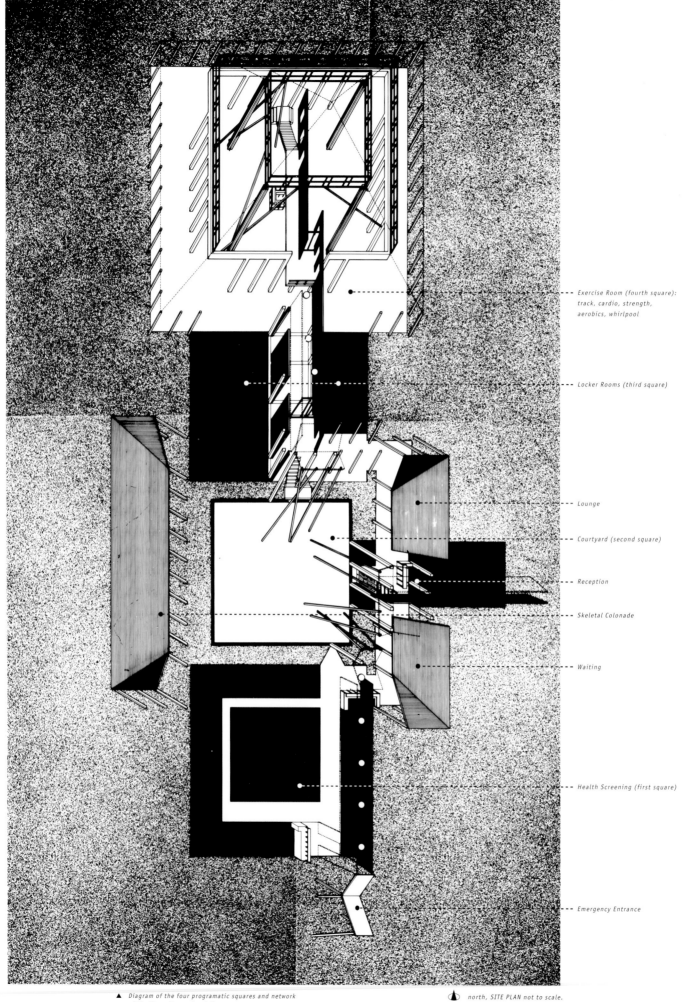

Exercise Room (fourth square):
track, cardio, strength,
aerobics, whirlpool

Locker Rooms (third square)

Lounge

Courtyard (second square)

Reception

Skeletal Colonade

Waiting

Health Screening (first square)

Emergency Entrance

▲ Diagram of the four programatic squares and network
of the three linear circulation spaces.

north, SITE PLAN not to scale.

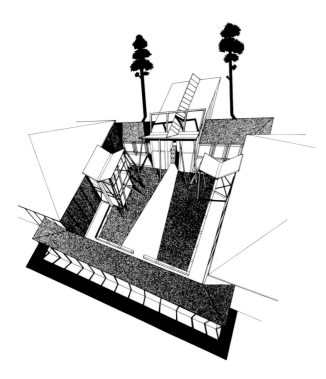

ently. The heart of the building is an open square, the courtyard. On either side of the court are "closed" squares: to the right, the health-screening clinic; to the left, the two-story lounge and exercise service areas. Beyond the two-story square is an "open/closed" square, the fourth and last in the series, housing the gym. This square is a pyramidal shed with full height glazing along the base and two rings of clerestory windows above.

Superimposed on the system of squares is the building's inter-nal circulation, a network of three linear spaces, for which the "open" square of the courtyard serves as a visual anchor. A visitor enters the center through a skele-tal colonnade separating the courtyard from the forest and the mill. Directly across the court-yard, through doors inscribed with the silhouette of the forest, is the first space, the entry hall. Once inside the visitor is led through this space to the other two linear spaces which open visually to the courtyard. One space serves as the main corridor of the screening building, one of the "solid" squares. The third cuts through the space of the workers' lounge, moves through the serv-ice areas, and then expands out-ward and upward to become the gym.

The forms of the surrounding southern architecture lend their innocence to the four squares. The grand front porch, the rustic stone house, the hip roofs, and the clerestory windows of the traditional barn are all here. The same ordinary and innocent elements are used over and over. ∎

▼ *The three major interior spaces—reception, employee lounge, and clinic waiting— originate in the entry courtyard under similar roof forms.*

EXIT

MONARK

▲ Window overlooking the courtyard from the waiting area in the clinic.

▲ The third linear circulation space, the balcony, extends up and out into the gym.

◄ The gym looking back toward the employee lounge.

▼ Axonometric view of the Health Center.

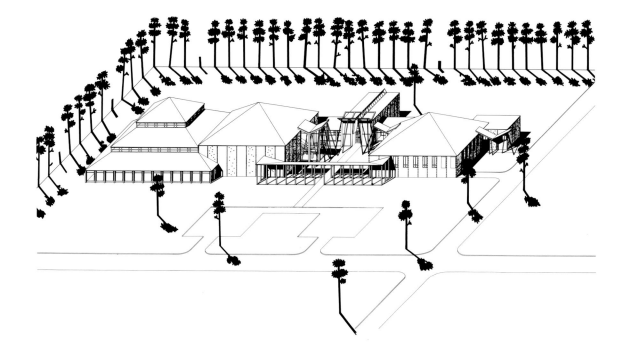

▲ *A single large blank panel, punctuated only by a small clock, dominate the eight columns defining the front face of the infill building. In front of the cylindrical form of the sanctuary, each column penetrates the skyline.*

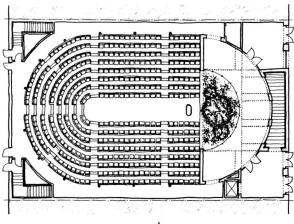

⚓ *north, FIRST FLOOR PLAN not to scale.*

CHURCH OF RELIGIOUS SCIENCE

designed for
Swanke Hayden Connell Architects
client
Church of Religious Science
site
Chicago, Illinois
designed
1985

Religious Science considers worship a matter of study and logic. The order of things is discovered through the process of education. The Church of Religious Science needed a new place for study and worship in Chicago. The project was never built.

The program principally consists of a sanctuary, which is similar to a Roman circus in plan. Parallel rows of seats face each other with one end closed in a semicircle. Everyone faces a lozenge-shaped platform from which the instructor addresses the congregation. No hierarchy is implied. A lower gallery for reception and circulation wraps around the taller sanctuary, filling the residual space within the boundaries of the site.

The building is an infill project on a vacant lot on Hubbard Street. A line of square columns modulates the street face. In the center, an enigmatic blank panel fills the space between the columns. The center is occupied, but we know not by what or by whom. The clock marks the ongoing enigma of the panel. People enter the building through the colonnade on either side of this panel. A circular excedra used for reception rises above the line of columns as it penetrates through the lower roof of the gallery space.

A blank panel, a clock, a line of square columns, and a cylinder, each is an innocent and easily understood object. But superimposed on one another, they are unexpected, raising more questions than they answer. ■

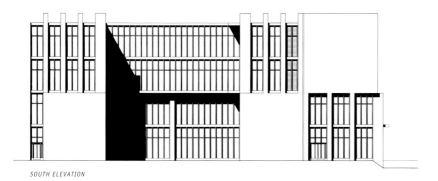

PILLSBURY RESEARCH AND DEVELOPMENT HEADQUARTERS

designed for
A. Epstein and Sons
International, Inc.
client
Pillsbury Companies
site
Minneapolis, Minnesota
designed
1986

The Pillsbury Companies' research and development facilities had been developed over time on an over-sized city block just across the river from downtown. Gradually, new buildings replaced old, with no overall plan in mind. The new head-quarters building was intended to solve two problems: first, it was to provide central facilities to serve the entire campus; and second, it was intended to reorganize the existing campus circulation pattern, which had become disorienting.

The skin of the building is a ver-tical lattice of aluminum, in-filled with glass. Identical elements are repeated, beginning at the ground and penetrating the roof planes. Anchoring elements of columns and blank panels are pulled from the spine toward the street. The alu-minum lattice stretches to fill the void. Simple uninformed elements are repeated over and over, their orientation changing, first right side up, then upside down.

The internal circulation within the new headquarters building extends across the back edge of the site. Horizontal circulation and adjacent stairs form the backbone of the campus connecting the head-quarters offices to the adjacent lab-oratory. The building is divided into two sections extending toward the street. The longer wing contains four levels of offices, while the shorter wing houses a two-story space for the food service operation and a two-level research library. ■

▲ *The site is surrounded on three sides by the blank walls of existing laboratory buildings, the headquarters building bisects the site in half defining two open courtyards, one paved and one green, opening to the street.*

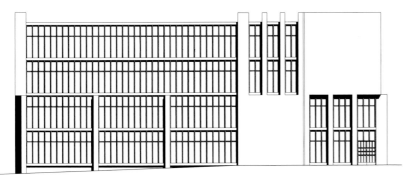

SOUTH ELEVATION

EAST ELEVATION

UNET MANUFACTURING FACILITY

client

3Com Corporation

site

Mount Prospect, Illinois

completed

1998

In its first life as the main factory for the leading manufacturer of mimeograph machines, this building was constructed in a series of phases until it covered 15 acres. For the most part the building was a shed, with the exception of the southern portions, which were a complicated mix of different additions completed over a long period of time to serve the administrative needs of the company. With the relentless advance of technological change, the mimeograph industry began to decline even as the final phases of construction were put in place. Soon the big shed was left abandoned.

This cast-off building was useful to both U.S. Robotics and its merger partner, 3Com Corporation. Needing a combined research and manufacturing facility for their Carrier Division to provide communications equipment to Internet Service Providers, the big shed offered a large platform with few fixed constraints responding to the changing and unpredictable needs of the rapidly growing company.

Where the existing shell met the requirements of the new program, most everything was left in place. But along the south edge, the office additions were scrapped away exposing the straight southern edge of the shed. This edge is marked by a new elevation composed of a regular repeated grid. The grid is modulated, changing in material and transparency, to accommodate remnants of the original

▲ A steel potato chip marks the reception area along the south facade, both on the interior and exterior of the building.

◄ The uniform module of the south face is defined by either brick or steel frames. The frames are filled with either glass, brick, or wire mesh. These changes reflect different interior uses, planning constraints, or existing conditions.

construction and new interior uses inserted under the old roof.

Within the old shed, the entire southern third of the building has been turned over to both administrative and research and development uses. In these areas the shed was stripped down to the structural frame, mezzanines were added, and all the building systems replaced, including the exterior skin. Organizing this redeveloped 5-acre zone is a two-story space lighted by square monitors puncturing the old roof. Running north-south, this linear atrium visually anchors the adjacent offices and labs.

The old both coexists and contrasts with the new. When convenient, the original factory remains, in some cases hardly changed. When necessary, new solutions are laid over the old patterns. ■

◄ *Each of the three bridges connect the upper level office areas which are separated by the two story clerestory space.*

◄◄ *Each of the three bridges is paired with a stair below and is supported by a bowstring truss.*

▲ *One of thirteen clerestory windows which bring light into the center of the research facility.*

▲ *Important nodes and service areas used by the entire staff are marked in the interior by dense frames of red wood.*

COMFORT A GUILTY PLEASURE

▲ Three Flags *by Jasper Johns, 1958. 30 7/8 x 45 1/2 x 5 inches, encaustic on canvas. 50th Anniversary Gift of the Gilman Foundation, Inc., The Lauder Foundation, A. Alfred Taubman, an anonymous donor and purchase. © Jasper Johns/Licensed by VAGA, New York, NY. Photographic Copyright © 1995: WHITNEY MUSEUM OF AMERICAN ART, NEW YORK. Photo by Geoffrey Clements.*

In science fiction, time travelers always carry their values as baggage. They never can view the worlds they visit in the same way as residents of these worlds. People of the twentieth century cannot escape from their time, though they often long to travel to an imagined past, not out of a genuine search for history, but rather to limit the sense of uncertainty. The past is fixed and comfortable in its certainty. Focusing on the past discourages any innovation, which might upset these associations. The future is more uncertain and filled with risk. But the future invites innovation.

To live with uncertainty, people need the pleasures of comfortable buildings. This sense of comfort should embrace change and innovation, and should not depend on memories of the past. The visual elasticity of the urban street is one place where almost anything is possible. The inhabitants of the street can play catch, practice their religion, exercise their civil rights, and engage in various vocations and avocations. There is

comfort in opportunity to do the unexpected—to invent and innovate. The urban street avoids answers, accepting all forms of unruly and disobedient behavior. These actions change the street by increments every day, leaving just enough behind to seem vaguely familiar and comfortable. Yet over time it becomes a completely new place. Instead of maintaining the past, there is comfort in the urban street as it changes incrementally, remaining familiar, while accepting opportunities of the new and unexpected.

The suburban street stands in contrast to its urban counterpart. The tightly defined and artificially ordered suburban street represents the lessons learned from the larger community. Civic order must be maintained. Lawns must be mowed, houses painted in sympathetic colors, and all activities relegated to the backyard in order to maintain the discipline of the message. Most recently, underscoring this air of artificiality, unused front porches have been added to the empty stage set. In the

96

discipline of the suburban community, a false comfort is found which bans innovation and the unexpected.

The discipline of the suburban street taken to an extreme is the fully controlled and enhanced imagery of the shopping mall. Added to the domestic bliss of rows of quaint homes and tailored green lawns are other marketing themes of rainforests, submarines, planets, and the ever-present myth of the frontier. In these highly symbolic environments, everything is distorted to support the theme. Anything that diffuses the illusion is banished. A singular, cohesive message results. Almost everyone gets the idea, making it possible to imagine that almost anything can be comfortable, including life in a log cabin, a jungle, or any other customarily forbidding environment. The effort that is required to maintain these illusions suggests that the modern American mind is distinctly unruly and undisciplined. The meaning of most places in the U.S. is very slippery and changeable.

In place of a coherent narrative, the very uncertainty of what a building means can be the root of its value. A building can be a catalyst for the imagination, like the urban street, where the contradictions and confusion are embraced, taking into account people's innocence, which makes the imagination both undisciplined and easily susceptible to suggestion.

When Jasper Johns painted *Three Flags*, he took one of the few widely accepted symbols of the U.S., the flag, and placed three in decreasing size, one on top of the other. This superimposition transformed the flag into an image that transcends the original meaning of the root symbol and suggests a missing narrative. The image resonates; it is new and unexpected, yet familiar and comfortable.

The most innovative buildings are often drawn from the most familiar and comfortable images. But these buildings are also unexpected and never fully explained. Often, a new thought is accepted because it refers to something inaccurately remembered. Inundated with non-essential information, more is forgotten than is remembered. A floor plan is recalled, but the hierarchies are forgotten, leading to new spatial relationships. A roof form is remembered, but the scale is distorted, resulting in an entirely different and unexpected building. A fish becomes a lamp; a lamp becomes a building. This could be the process leading from a fish to Frank Gehry's Fish Lamp for Formica's Forms and Surfaces exhibition and eventually to the decidedly organic forms of Gehry's Bilbao Guggenheim Museum. Architecture should be derivative, and therefore, it can be familiar.

Such architecture depends on our innocence; our absent and failed memories are highly suggestive. There can be comfort without memories. Clapboard siding, brick coursing, strip fluorescent lights, or avocado colors provide only the mildest suggestions, making a building seem familiar. The narrative should remain incomplete, leaving a full understanding of the idea up to the imagination of the individual.

As the unknown is derived from the known, our innocence remembers only the opportunities accompanying change, forgetting the difficulties, making us comfortable. This also suggests that those acts of civil disobedience, important to innovation, should be accepted. There is comfort in the unexpected. Buildings can be both vaguely familiar and unexpected at the same time. Such buildings are both innovative and comfortable. ■

▲ The administrative building sits at the edge of the palm court and serves as the front door for the entire complex.

◄ The library building is at the end of the entry axis from the palm court.

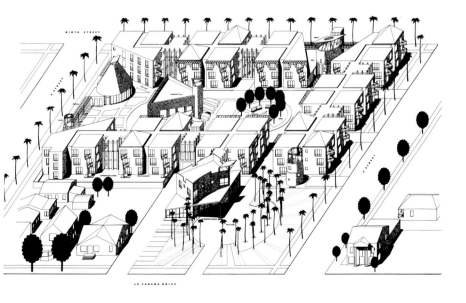

COLTON PALMS
APARTMENTS

client
Cooperative Services, Inc.
site
Colton, California
completed
1991

The site is at the center of the City of Colton, "Hub of Industry," a town on the edge of Los Angeles. A vacant parcel of land in the old downtown was selected by the city for redevelopment as affordable housing for seniors. Single family homes seemingly inspired by Irving Gill, or in other cases the Greene Brothers, dominate in the area. Frank Benest, the city manager, expected the unexpected—a housing development which was both comfortable and innovative. To this end, the city, working with the not-for-profit developer Cooperative Services Inc.,

sponsored an international
design competition.

As a basic design objective of
the premiated solution, the fabric and scale of Colton is recalled
by the pattern of objects that
make up the hundred-unit project. The streets, sidewalks, and
parks of the old town work-
experience has tested the look
and feel of the old town and
finds no reason for a change.

The site plan starts as a nine
square; each square is a three-
story cluster of nine to twelve
apartments, with the center
square removed for a green.
The fabric of the nine square is
extended to the north and to
the east, and carved away in
places, making room for landmark "public" buildings—the
meeting hall, library, crafts
pavilion, and the entry buildings. The palm court is an extension of Fleming Park, just across
the street. The Park is a WPA
project laid out in the 1930s.

Colton Palms embodies many
of the principles of New Urbanism
that have been used to plan new
"old comfortable" towns like
Celebration, Florida. "Public"
buildings have separate civic iden-
tities and have been placed to
punctuate the carefully scaled and
detailed clusters of homes.
Although using similar planning
principles, Colton Palms avoids

◄ *A curved face of the administra-*
tion building follows the line
defined by the circle of palms
at the entry. The library is seen
on axis in the distance.

PALM COURT

COMMUNITY GREEN

picturesque imagery. The visual cues are purposely vague and ambiguous, playing on a memory of some time or some place that most of the citizens of Colton left behind long ago. The seniors who live in Colton are more connected to the wide-eyed optimism of the postwar future than any imagined memory of nineteenth-century small-town America. The functional plan, similar to the towns based on the New Urbanism, has proved useful in defining a community for a unique population for whom a slower, pedestrian lifestyle has replaced the speed of their younger years. ■

◀ A stair wraps around the library building reaching a bridge connecting the apartments at the third floor level.

◀◀ A disk inscribed on the triangular plan of the community hall forms a canopy over its three main doors.

▲ The cylindrical enclosure for one of the fire stairs is seen in the distance from the administrative offices.

▶ Seen from the main doors, the interior of the community hall is a triangle overlaid on a circle.

ADMINISTRATIVE BUILDING

COMMUNITY HALL

CRAFT BUILDING

BLOCK 89 MULTIUSE DEVELOPMENT

client
Urban Land Interests
site
Madison, Wisconsin
anticipated completion
1999

Capitol Square is the most important public space in the state of Wisconsin. The context of the square played a key role in the redevelopment of Block 89, one of the eight city blocks which bound the square. The Block 89 designation comes from the original plan of the city. To develop an approach to the design, there first had to be a clear understanding of the history of this place. The capitol building, typical of many nineteenth-century government buildings, was intended to dominate the Madison skyline.

In comparison, the surrounding buildings were small, typically a single lot in width. In some cases, lots were assembled and larger multistory structures were built. But the overall character was clear—many small buildings, each with its own individual entrepreneurial identity, competing with one another for attention. The energy and complexity of these surrounding buildings contrasted sharply with the strength and monumentality of the capitol building. It is this contrast between individual entrepreneurship and

▲ *The brick grid along the structural columns bevels away from the street.*

▶ *The fabric of brick ripples as it turns the corner of Doty and Pinckney streets.*

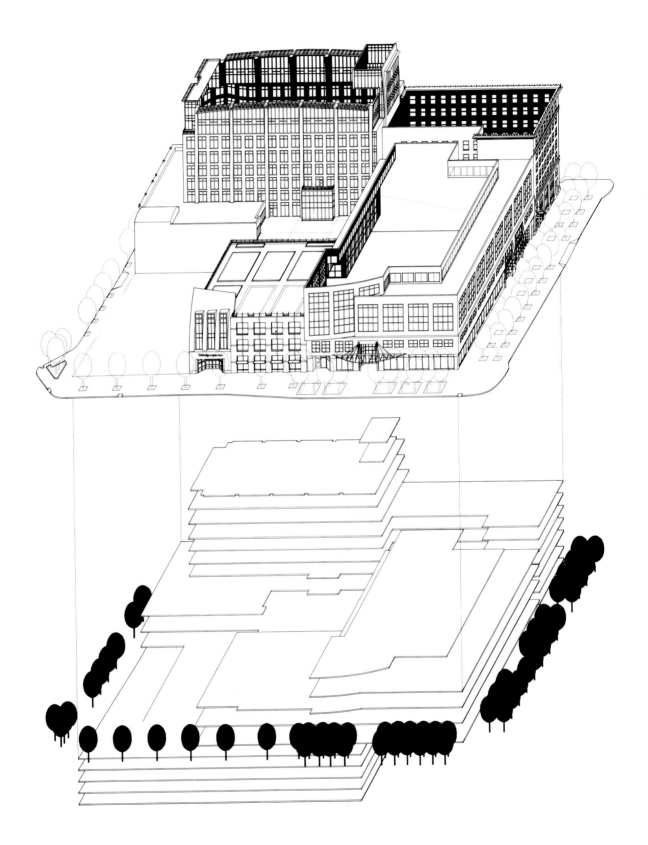

▲ Exploded axonometric as seen from the State Capitol Building.

the expression of the will of the people which gave the square its unique character.

In the recent past, the character of the square has been changed through the construction of several monumental corporate buildings. These structures threaten the visual tradition of the area. Reversing this trend, the redevelopment of Block 89 lays an imagined pattern of "lot lines" over the property. The elevations facing the streets were developed as a series of different facades; each considers the height, materials, and character of its neighbor in some different way. Instead of a monumental image featuring a single amplified voice, Block 89 is a chorus of different voices. The capitol building is left to dominate the square, while each object rubs up against its neighbor, straining for attention, comfortable in the understanding that this is a competition between equals.

Except for two buildings all of the existing buildings on the one block site of Block 89 were removed. The facade of a two-story historic building was disas-

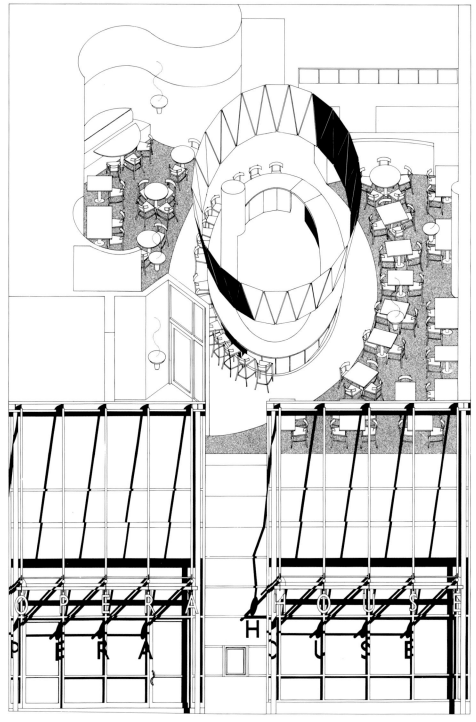

▲ The aluminum and glass wall forms a transparent screen connecting the street and the monumental fan of the bar in the Opera House Restaurant.

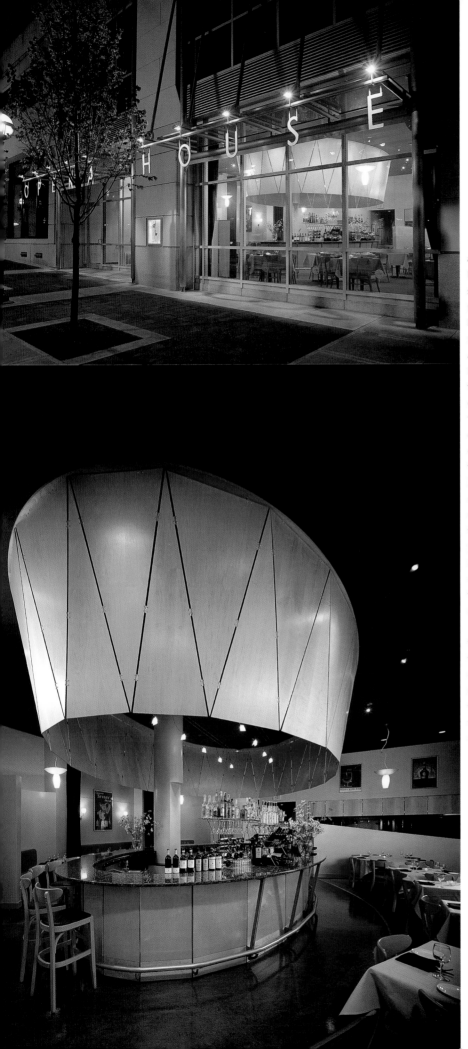

assembled and warehoused for later reinstallation around a new structural frame. A new five-story parking deck was excavated below grade, on top of which the new buildings were constructed. A new four-story retail and office building was constructed facing the square, its facade broken down into a series of smaller "buildings" that recall the small entrepreneurial buildings that once surrounded the square. A ten-story office building was built on the side of the block opposite the square, its top modulated to bring a smaller scale to the Madison skyline than the corporate monuments nearby. The buildings on the block have been organized to share a common infrastructure of loading docks, elevators, and stairs.

Maintaining a traditional scale is not a question of style. Some things are remembered while others are forgotten, making Block 89 both appropriate for the late twentieth century and composed to recall the entrepreneurial scale of the area. ■

▲ *The Opera House Restaurant bar can be seen from the street through the curtainlike glass facade.*

◄ *Titanic in scale, the elliptical bar is the focus of the restaurant.*

▲ *Engaged in a never-ending dialogue, the new addition on the left is
the idealized twin of the old farm house on the right.*

GRIFFITH HOUSE

client
Gary and Carol Griffith
site
Hubertus, Wisconsin
completed
1984

The existing building is a 60-year-old wood-frame farmhouse, ordinary in almost every respect. The addition "doubles" the existing building, repeating the shape of the vernacular house as a second, carefully composed architectural form. The value of the old is enhanced by its affect on the new. The value of the new form is increased by its perfection in comparison to the old. The familiar vernacular and the academic stand in comfortable contrast to one another.

The most suggestive buildings often are often vaguely drawn from the most common images. Although the architecture is based on a traditional image, duplicating the form disrupts any connections to the past. The ordinary becomes exceptional through repetition. ■

SELF-EVIDENCE

The appeal to self-evidence did not displace more academic and more dogmatic modes of thinking among Americans, but American life nourished it until it became a prevailing mode. It was not the system of a few great American Thinkers, but the mood of Americans thinking. It rested on two sentiments. The first was a belief that the reasons men give for their actions are much less important than the actions themselves, that it is better to act well for wrong or unknown reasons than to treasure a systemized "truth" with ambiguous conclusions, that deep reflection does not necessarily produce the most effective action. The second was a belief that the novelties of experience must be freely admitted into men's thought. Why strain the New World through the philosophical sieves of the Old? If philosophy denied the innuendoes of experience, the philosophy—not the experience—must be rejected. Therefore, a man's mind was wholesome not when it possessed the most refined implements for dissecting and ordering all knowledge, but when it was most sensitive to the unpredicted whisperings of the environment. It was less important that the mind be elegantly furnished than that it be open and unencumbered.[1]

DANIEL J. BOORSTIN

▲ *Zzyzx Road exit at the abandoned utopian community of the same name, located somewhere in the desert between Los Angeles and Las Vegas.*

Among most architects, buildings that can be explained are preferred, but an elegant theory is less important than a building, which resonates in the mind. Those "unpredicted whisperings of the environment" are often the most important noises a building makes. Often the most appropriate buildings are inexplicable.

But the intent of most buildings is to make very little "noise." They are expected to harmonize with their neighbors, repeating the same plot lines, composed of recognizable imagery. Any aberrations are purposely stamped out. Nothing is questioned, nothing is missing. Yet the glue that binds us to these traditions is weak. Change occurs frequently, replacing the expected with the unexpected. Among most architects, innovations that can be explained are preferred.

Architects expect the image and other qualities of a new building to be developed based on carefully constructed and coherent thoughts. The academic argument is expected to dominate over intuition and experience. In this process change occurs by heroic act, such as Alberti inventing a new architecture in the pages of his *Ten Books of Architecture*. The explanation precedes the construction.

There is an alternative to this academic process. Innovation can be the by-product of experience.

There is nothing new in this approach to invention, yet this method is at times considered accidental. It is just different, dependent on the "accreting" ways of many people: "diffused, elusive, process oriented" were the words Boorstein used to describe innovation in America. This approach to architecture can be compared to the sciences, where the existence of something that cannot be seen can be measured based on its influence on other phenomena that can be seen. The process is deductive in science while it is intuitive in building. The construction is based on the logic of the process, while the explanation is left for another time. Such an intuitive process does not decrease the importance of the invention.

In one case the innovation is explained by testing the building against the logic of the philosophy. But buildings based on a concise manifesto can become self-referential, becoming more concerned with the question "can this be explained?", as opposed to "does this work?" For the architect the effort to align a building with a theory imposes the discipline of completing the thought and reaching a conclusion. By implication the narrative is complete.

An intuitive process encourages us to test our conclusions repeatedly. At the same time it frees us to leave questions unanswered. The intuitive process begins with something that is known; logic transforms the known to something both derivative and wholly unexpected.

A significant example is the Low House by McKim, Mead & White. Stanford White had designed a series of shingle-style houses derived from the Stoughton House by H. H. Richardson. Each of these buildings had evolved from the precedent using simple yet massive geometric forms, and sheathed in a taut skin of cedar shingles; the geometric shapes lost their mass

and appeared almost weightless. The Low House was the conclusion of this process of derivation and invention. The building pulled all the programmed spaces together under one huge gabled roof, its mass contradicted by the shingled skin. The resulting form appeared remarkably modern, and has been recognized as critical in Robert Venturi's design for his mother's house.

Driven by the process, beginning with the Stoughton House, the evolution ended in the Low House. This building is both derivative and wholly unexpected. No philosophy could precisely predict this building; its design is self-evident. Imbedded in the architecture of the Low House is a certain freedom and spontaneity. The origins of the design are in part indeterminate. Something that is indeterminate can imply a missing narrative.

Two different approaches to innovation have been defined; one based, first, on theory, while the other is based on intuition and experimentation. In either case, the new replaces the old. With either approach, the willingness to accept change must be supported by experience. To paraphrase Boorstin, if the philosophy denies the conclusions of the experience, then the philosophy, not the experience, should be rejected.

In a place like the U.S., where the inertia of history and the past is weak, constant change leads to exceptions and contradictions. Intellectual theory usually attempts to make the contradictory rational, stumbling over the exceptions. In contrast, the principles underlying the Low House are self-evident. Architecture has moved from the expected to the unexpected in understandable steps. The building is innovative, yet the architecture remains unexplained and indeterminate. Such buildings can make a great deal of noise, resonating with the population. ■

U 2
MANUFACTURING
FACILITY

client
U.S. Robotics Corporation
site
Skokie, Illinois
completed
1992

In the 1940s, hundreds of factory buildings were built in Chicago with strip-windowed masonry facades. Behind these skins were stick frames, often with wooden trusses—truly a nineteenth-century structural solution behind a twentieth-century face. The vagaries of the real estate market led U.S. Robotics to purchase one such building and convert it to their first electronics plant in the Midwest.

The plan is organized as a series of layers beginning with the exterior wall, followed by open office areas, circulation, private offices, and finally the

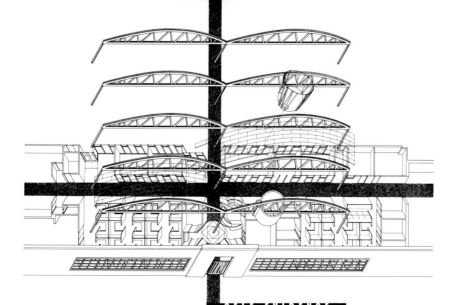

▲ *In the original construction a column was placed on the centerline of the front door. A steel ring orbits this column in the reception area making an accident of design a celebrated condition.*

◄ *Axonometric diagram.*

production zones. The geometry of the existing structural grid unexpectedly places a column on the centerline of the front door. The structural module contradicts the sense of entry. To celebrate this contradiction the column is orbited by a steel ring. From this origin a highly rational, orthogonal circulation plan evolves, always placing a structural column at each intersection. The building evolves from what was there originally. A new order is accepted as a context for innovation. ■

▶ *The arch of the ceiling is extended by suspended panels seen from within the steel ring at the entry.*

▶▶ *The ceiling of the main conference room is carved up to expose the bowstring truss which passes through a glass surface opening onto the reception area.*

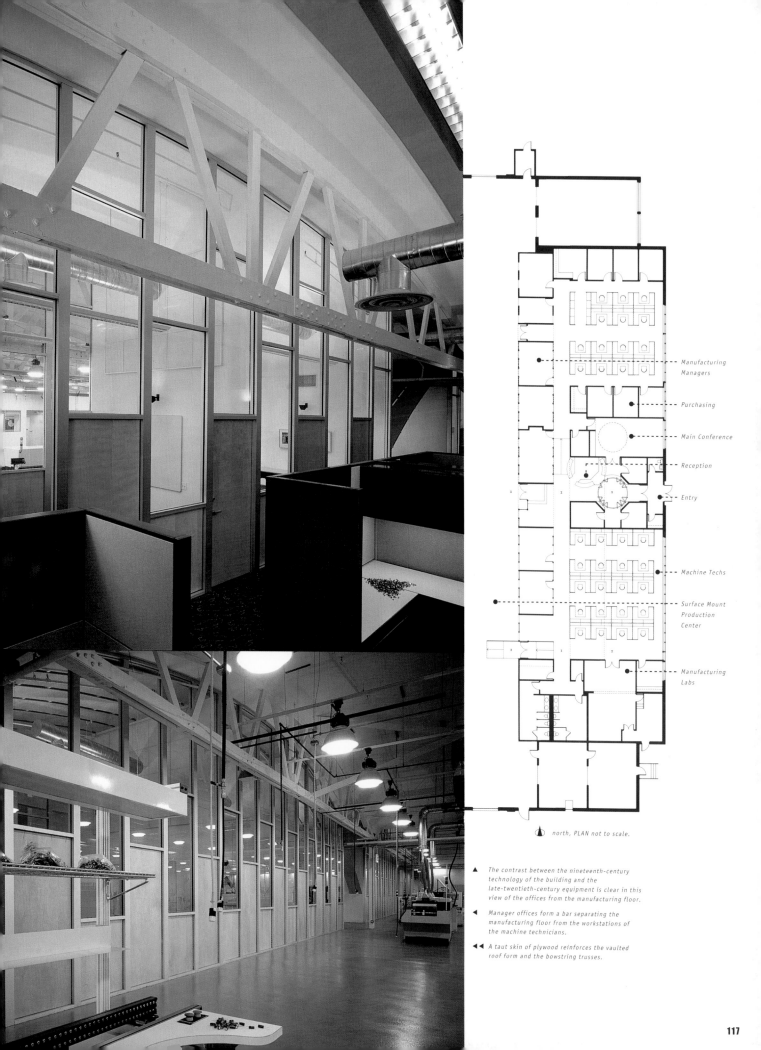

Manufacturing
Managers

Purchasing

Main Conference

Reception

Entry

Machine Techs

Surface Mount
Production
Center

Manufacturing
Labs

north, PLAN not to scale.

▲ The contrast between the nineteenth-century
technology of the building and the
late-twentieth-century equipment is clear in this
view of the offices from the manufacturing floor.

◀ Manager offices form a bar separating the
manufacturing floor from the workstations of
the machine technicians.

◀◀ A taut skin of plywood reinforces the vaulted
roof form and the bowstring trusses.

▲ The two levels of the office are connected by a two-story space at the center.

◀ The grid of workstations with their stainless-steel demising panels are
modulated to the same frequency as the column grid of the building.

OFFICES FOR WMA CONSULTING ENGINEERS, LTD.

site
Chicago, Illinois
completed
1996

Engineers take themselves seriously: they guard rational thought in an increasingly ambiguous world. The offices for WMA Consulting Engineers are based on the development of an individual workstation. To a mechanical engineer there are basic needs which are self-evident, a norm which can be applied to every engineer in the firm. Each station is designed to provide a tight and efficient workplace. From this basic component the module is

mirrored and mirrored again to form a grid of blocks and streets which were inserted into the first and second floors of a nineteenth-century loft building in Chicago.

At the edges of the matrix, the module evolves to form large semiprivate offices and even larger private offices. In plan, everything seems ordered and necessary. In the third dimension, everything is an exception. The main building services of lighting, HVAC, and sprinklers are planned

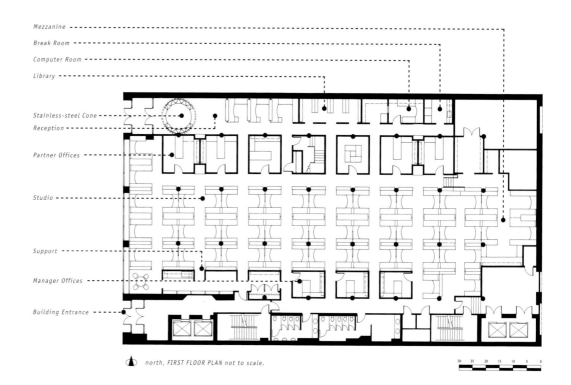

Mezzanine -

Break Room -

Computer Room -

Library -

Stainless-steel Cone - - - - -

Reception - - - - - - -

Partner Offices - - - - - -

Studio - - - - - - -

Support - - - - - - -

Manager Offices - - - - - -

Building Entrance - - - - - -

north, *FIRST FLOOR PLAN* not to scale.

30 25 20 15 10 5 0

▲ From the Wabash Street entrance, the office is reached through a
faceted stainless-steel cone.

◄ The cone, as seen from the reception area.

on contrasting, sometimes diago-
nal, grids. The private office
enclosures, so bland in plan,
become buildinglike icons
extending vertically through the
second floor, dotted with a dia-
mond grid of implied windows.

At the entry is the major
exception—an inverted conical
drum which is the transition from
the zone of the street to the zone
of the office. Is it a remnant from
some long-forgotten duct passing
through the space? By coinci-

dence the pie-shaped sections
forming the cone also form the
letters "W," "M," and "A" over and
over again.

Everything begins with the
workstation. The logic of the workstation is self-evident. From this
beginning, the plan and elevations
evolve as one logical step after
another. Each new element refers
to some other element. It is all
seems necessary—a comforting
thought for the rational mind. ■

MODULAR FACTORY

client
The Mobile Communications Division of 3Com Corporation

site
Salt Lake City, Utah

completed
1997

All the notebook computers in the world need a modem to communicate with the Internet. The technology of choice is a PC card, the size of a business card, about as thick as a quarter. These devices slip into a slot in the side of the computer. The largest manufacturer of these cards is the Mobile Communications Division of U.S. Robotics Corporation in Salt Lake City, Utah.

The explosive growth of this business prompted the construction of a new building next to the old facility. As soon as programming was complete, sales projections increased and the manufacturing managers wondered if the factory was big enough. To facilitate growth of the building, the plant is planned as a series of layers, measuring 40 feet in width from north to south, and 440 feet in length. There are eleven of these layers in all, defining a building of 165,000 square feet. The site allows for the addition of up to six additional layers to the north.

Beginning along the south facade, the first layer is two stories and houses office functions. This layer is only 280 feet in

▲ *The entrance canopy is the punctuation mark at the end of building's south face.*

◄ *An elliptical shape is used to define the reception desk and adjacent stair connecting the two levels of offices.*

▲ From the upper level, the glass wall separates the production floor from the workstations for the machine technicians.

◄ The south face of building is composed of three layers: the cantilevered screens, the glass curtain wall, and a wire-mesh ceiling.

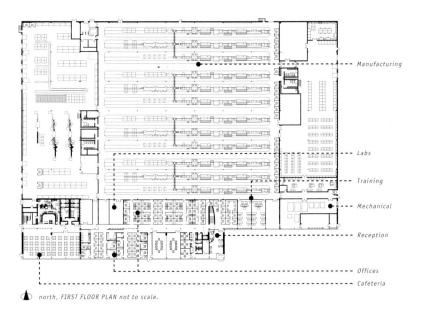

Manufacturing

Labs

Training

Mechanical

Reception

Offices

Cafeteria

north, FIRST FLOOR PLAN not to scale.

length, allowing for expansion to the west. The next layer is a service zone, with workstations for manufacturing managers, training rooms, mechanical rooms, food service, and other functions that support either the production floor or the office zone. The remaining nine layers are all identical, with each module designed to house two automated surface mount technology production lines.

In a building that is more than anything else linear and horizontal, what can be considered significant? The answer is not found in some carefully considered philosophy. Instead the nature of the program is primary. The answer exists in the fundamental dynamics of the building; the linear elements are accepted, then strengthened, making the horizontal monumental in scale. All the bits and pieces of industrial

hardware have been stretched, attenuated, and elongated until each appears as a taut band running from one end of each module to the other.

Where the building's dynamics demand change, an occasional contradiction creeps into view insuring a certain level of disturbance in the perfection of the production cycle. On the exterior the flying canopy defines the location of the door. On the interior, an elliptical form is traced on the floor and then projected vertically; one half of the ellipse defines the stair and bridge, providing access to the second floor, while the other half shapes the space occupied by the receptionist. These elements are anchors for the anonymity of the rational requirements of the building, intentionally disturbing the laminar flow of the monumental horizontals. ■

BALTIMORE
BRIDGES

designed jointly with
Kent Hubbell
client
Inner Harbor
Development Project
site
Baltimore, Maryland
completed
1981

Three bridges connect the old
piers in Baltimore's Inner
Harbor Development District.
The bridges are part of a larger
retail and entertainment complex intended to revitalize the
entire harbor front. Each bridge
is covered with a thin membrane
stretched over a frame of struts,
arches, and cables. The surface
could remind someone of the
skin covering the vertebrae of
the spine, smooth and bumpy at
the same time. The tension in
the skin denies the visual mass;
the compressive form of the
arch denies the tension of the
surface. Yet image and structure
cannot be separated, making
the form both self-evident and
ambiguous. ■

Baltimore Bridges

Old Power Plant

Baltimore Bridges

National Aquarium

◄ *Three bridges connect the fingers
of landmasses which extend into
the harbor.*

▲ *Light is reflected up from the water
and is modulated by the doubly
curved surface of the canopy.*

▲▲ *The power plant is the backdrop
for one of the three pedestrian
bridges.*

north, SITE PLAN not to scale.

▲ Isle of California *by the LA Fine Arts Squad (Victor Henderson and Terry Schoonhoven), 1971-72 on the Village Recorder, formally the Masonic Temple.*

am-big-u-ous   adj. 1. having several possible meanings or interpretations. 2. difficult to comprehend, distinguish, or classify. 3. lacking clearness or definiteness; n, obscure; indistinct.[1]

THE RANDOM HOUSE COLLEGE DICTIONARY

In the relentlessly modern U.S., will the same building ever be understood by different people in the same way? Or will every building be ambiguous, open to different interpretations over time? This capacity to define and then redefine the same image is what it means to be modern. In spite of the use of any precedents or the logic of any theories, different people will see different things in the same building. Even the same person will see different things in the same building over time. This is the case whether a building is old or just looks old, is new or looks new. To modern people all buildings have a modern meaning. As an illustration, consider two buildings with different design intentions.

One is based on traditional architectural intentions. It is an expression of a carefully considered philosophy. It may be an older building built in an earlier style. Or it may be a new building based on some theory of historicism. Similar traditional intentions also apply to much of modern architecture. A building may appear rational, suggesting that rationalism is an ideal; or it may be chaotic, implying that order does not exist or that order is extremely difficult to understand. The image may vary, but the motive remains the same: to carefully design the building to support a theory connecting intent and image.

In this first example, the architecture implies a specific narrative. But our rootlessness and absence of a shared history, and all the reasons that we have cited, make people unequipped to understand the building's narrative. Instead, people provide their own interpretations. The building is ambiguous in spite of itself.

The second building is both ordinary and unexpected. It is an innocent idea, independent from any expected ordering system. If convenient, its image may borrow forms from any source. The building reminds everyone of something, but the memory is fuzzy and not specific. The architecture is derivative; the design has evolved from the known moving toward the unknown. There is a logic in this process that can be explained, and based on this logic the solution appears to be self-evident. On some levels the building is understandable, with links going back to some starting point. Because it is both familiar and self-evident, the building is comfortable.

The building is also completely unexpected. In this second example the architecture has evolved from a known starting point to an unknown conclusion. The design is self-evident, resting on its own internal logic. But as a result it is freed from the need to refer to any specific theory or visual context. With this freedom, contradictions are allowed to multiply. The building

as a whole is incomplete and cannot be explained. For those who are innocent of the past and the lessons of history, there is a confidence in the unexpected and the unknown. Innocence expects a philosophy of the unexpected; architecture that can never be fully understood is difficult to both miss and dismiss. Like Cindy Sherman's *Film Stills*, or Jasper Johns's *Three Flags*, the building implies a missing narrative for anyone to complete. This second building is purposely ambiguous and indeterminate.

Both buildings are ambiguous. Both are modern because the people who use them are modern. In the first case this is by accident. Whatever the image, either historic or modern, the architect's carefully crafted narrative cannot be understood. In this case ambiguity is the end point. The second example is modern by intention. Its architecture is suggestive and purposely not specific, encouraging as many different interpretations as there are people. In this second example, ambiguity is the point of departure.

Helen Frankenthaler painted *Mountains and Sea* in 1952. This painting is one of a series of her paintings that contrasted exposed canvas against areas of flowing and overlapping colors. The exposed canvas implies uncertainty, openness, and a sense of being incomplete.

Like Frankenthaler's painting, there are an infinite number of ways to leave the "canvas" of a building exposed. The enigmatic blank panel dominating the facade of Le Corbusier's Villa Schwob in La Chaux-de-Fonds is literally Frankenthaler's exposed canvas. Clearly something is missing from the blank panel dominating the street-front facade, and no one is there to complete the narrative.

In other cases unexpected ambiguity results when two different narratives collide. The Los Angeles Fine Arts Squad painted the *Isle of California*, an image of the California coast after Los Angeles has fallen into the Pacific Ocean, on the alley facade of an old building in Culver City. The old building is an object in the finest tradition of nineteenth-century architecture, with plinth, pilasters, and cornice. The painting defines the illusion of three-dimensional space. When space and object share the same corner of the building, the effect is ambiguity.

Ambiguity is often the intention in recent architecture. Sometimes it is loud and obvious, while at other times it is subtle. One of Frank Gehry's most resonant buildings is the West Hollywood Library. The structure is undistinguished and ordinary, except for two exaggerated cubes teetering over the edge of the otherwise expected facade. The two objects imply any number of unwritten stories. In some cases, Colonial architecture demonstrates a comfort with ambiguity. Robert Venturi, in *Complexity and Contradiction in Architecture*, noticed that the arrangement of windows on the otherwise symmetrical land-side facade of Mount Vernon formed an asymmetrical pattern. No attempt is made to apply remedies, allowing the pattern to contradict the overall form. It is unexpected and contradictory.

Our buildings are comfortable with their contradictions and ambiguities. Things that are impossibly thin, or impossibly heavy, contradict people's expectations. The cantilevered stair in our Gardner Apartment is fabricated from a single bent plate of 3/16-inch-thick aluminum. With no visible means of support, it is unexplained. The same is true of unexplained differences when similar forms are juxtaposed or aligned, but differ in some important quality. In our very small Griffith House, the form of the old Dutch farmhouse is mimicked by a new addition. The two objects stand facing one another—one vernacular with messy asymmetries, the other perfect in its geometry. They are similar, but their differences are not explained, leaving their meanings open-ended.

In modern building, we believe ambiguity should always be the starting point. Ambiguity is necessarily the product of designs that are incomplete and indeterminate, implying a missing narrative. A building lacking a narrative erases traditional understandings and interpretations, and is in a way innocent. Architecture should embrace ambiguity. ■

▲ The south face of the building is highly disciplined in its lack of discipline.

◄ The campus master plan includes six major buildings and four parking structures. Only Phase One has been completed and occupied.

INTERSTATE 90

INTERSTATE 290

Future Office Buildings

Future Parking Structures (typical)

Phase One (complete)

Future Office Buildings

⊿ north, PLAN not to scale.

GOLF ROAD

MIDWEST CORPORATE CAMPUS

client
3Com Corporation

site
Rolling Meadows, Illinois

completed
1998

Driving in from Iowa on the interstate, the traveler passes a sign for Chicago, and then, off to the right, sees a long line of monolithic, green panels. First one leans in, then another leans out, and then groups rock back and forth, repeating the same movement. The panels are like the bones of a whale cast up on the beach. Big and wide, the skeleton is easily read at highway speed as cars drive past. So this is Chicago, the traveler thinks.

The master plan for 3Com's new regional center takes shape around an unused 400,000-square-foot building on a large

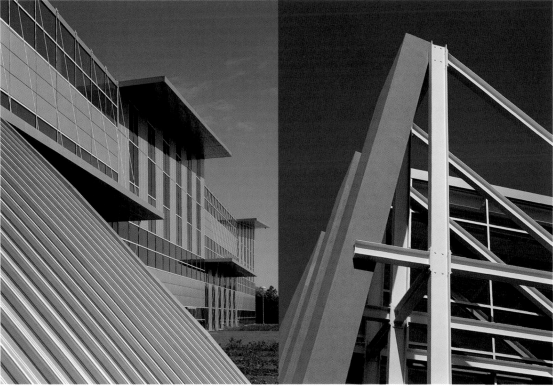

▲ *The south entry is the principal entrance for visitors.*

◄ *The steel structure defining the entry is an extension of the structure enclosing the interior street.*

◄◄ *Four canopies separate the south facade into a composition of components oriented either vertically or horizontally.*

tract of land in the northwest suburbs of Chicago. The design strategy strips the skin off the existing building, resurfaces the entire exterior, and grafts on another floor plus a major interior street to create a 512,000-square-foot office building. Behind the monolithic precast panels is this new street, the first link of a new primary internal circulation spine connecting future buildings and parking structures to the parent building and its support spaces.

Unlike the buildings in its context, this new face is not meant to recede into the landscaped parking lots, but to be seen by a person in motion. The plasticity of the exterior wall system becomes an important contradiction. Wrapped around the other three sides of the building is a stretched skin of glass and aluminum. Other suburban office buildings pick a single orientation for their elevations: either vertical or horizontal. The decision is arbitrary. This building chooses both, exploring the evident ambiguity. Different orientations are layered one on top of the other until the floor lines are obscured and the height of the building becomes indeter-

▶ *Seen in the distance, the vaulted form of the reception area anchors the south entry.*

▼ *The composition of wall panels references the projecting roofs and vice versa, making the whole appear justified.*

minate. The building is blurred even when viewed at rest. The effect of speed only increases the overlapping of one thought on another.

The space of the interior street is a servant of the monolithic panels, just like the space of any city street is subordinate to the surrounding buildings. The edges of this street are defined by a series of "public" buildings: a tower of conference rooms, an elliptical frame enclosing a small cafe, the 3Com store, an auditorium, training center, cafeteria, and other functions. These buildings

▲ *The enclosure for the east entrance and stair are defined by two leaning brick panels.*

◄ *The east entrance is the main point of access for the staff.*

◄◄ *Detail.*

▲ The backbone of the entire campus is the west wall of the interior street,
   defined by a skeleton of precast concrete panels. These over-scaled monoliths
   are intended to be viewed fast from cars passing the site on I-290.

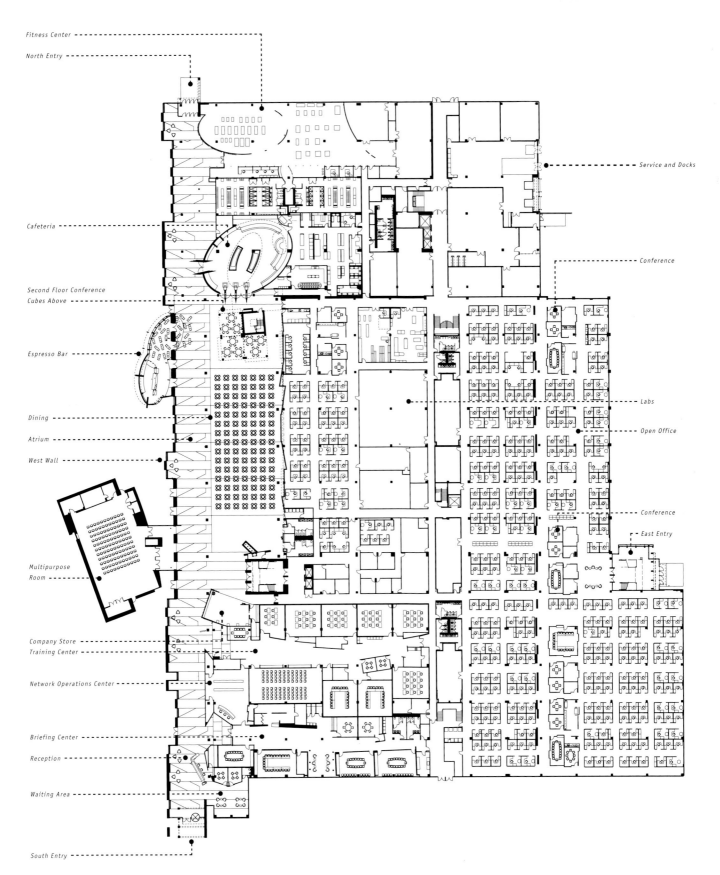

Fitness Center

North Entry

Cafeteria

Second Floor Conference
Cubes Above

Espresso Bar

Dining

Atrium

West Wall

Multipurpose
Room

Company Store
Training Center

Network Operations Center

Briefing Center

Reception

Waiting Area

South Entry

Service and Docks

Conference

Labs

Open Office

Conference

East Entry

north, FIRST FLOOR PLAN not to scale.

mediate between the speed of the big wall and the speed of a person walking by. Outside and inside, the building is a riot of forms and surfaces, all concerned with speed. The ordinary materials of the suburban office building come together in one place. Where these elements once made very few sounds, brought together in one building they make some noise.

This project is a collaborative effort with STUDIOS Architecture, whose responsibilities included the joint development of the campus plan and sole responsibility for the auditorium, executive briefing center, and training center. ■

▲ *The second floor conference center is defined by four cubes, each leaning away from the common center at a similar angle, but in four different directions.*

◀ *A brick panel floating free from the surrounding structure anchors the south entry.*

◀◀ *A line of concrete columns topped with steel trees support the roof of the interior street.*

▶ *The leaning walls of the clusters reference the precast panels of the west wall.*

▶▶ *A series of 24-foot clusters are scattered throughout the floor plan to house conference rooms, service areas and wiring centers. Smaller conference rooms, such as this one, use half or one-quarter of a cluster.*

▼ *The different activity zones in the fitness center are linked by a line of lighted columns.*

▲ Interior of the espresso bar looking out at I-290.

◄ In contrast to the over-scaled precast panels, the small scale of the espresso bar references the small scale and the speed of the pedestrian.

◄◄ The scale of the espresso bar is an intentional contrast to the large scale of the interior street.

▲ The office entry is shaped by a tilted surface covered with sheet vinyl.

◄ The reception desk is defined by a series of elliptical wood forms.

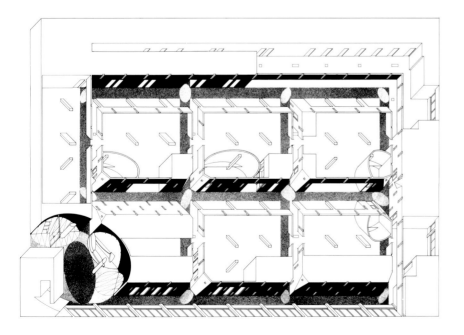

USTATE OFFICE AND RESEARCH CENTER

client
U.S. Robotics Corporation
site
Skokie, Illinois
completed
1993

The renovation project began with an ordinary suburban office building originally built for a large insurance company. The 135,000-square-foot, two-story structure was home to a relentless, staccato rhythm of desks for insurance adjusters. The pattern was reinforced by a grid of columns at 20-foot intervals.

To make the plan comprehensible, circulation corridors sliced the huge floor plate in both the east/west and north/south directions, organizing the infinite grid of columns into six large blocks of space on each level. These blocks were thought of as "inside," while the corridors were "outside." In the

▲ *"Streets" are defined between walls covered with a matrix of light slots.*

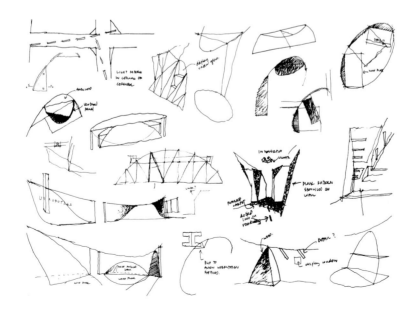

outdoor spaces, the old acoustical ceilings were "excavated" to expose the structural concrete deck overhead. Partitions and soffits were added to define offices and storage areas clustered along the corridors.

Where the old desks were once uncountable, the new workstations were finite, contained in six "buildings," each separated by an interior "street." A single, simple idea finds an urban landscape where only carpeting and desks existed before. The architecture is suggestive. But the corridors are not really "streets" and the blocks are not really "buildings." This is only one explanation for a design which is open to many possible interpretations. ■

▲ The stair moves up and through the glass surface as it passes
vertically through the house.

HERSHMAN/ REINHARD HOUSE

clients
Shirley and Seymour Hershman,
Keith and Rose Lee Reinhard
site
Chicago, Illinois
completed
1980

This Chicago home renovation now has two faces. The project starts with a nineteenth-century stone facade: solid, defensive, predictable—a good neighbor. Walking into the house, the visitor comes to the base of a second facade of glass. The impossibly thin, twentieth-century glass curtain wall cuts the building in half. The role of the first is obvious, while that of the second must be discovered.

The glass is inserted to mediate between front and back, public and private. It stretches from the skylight to the first floors almost 40 feet below. Within this slot of light, a stair converts the static grid of glass into a theatrical experience. Starting at the lowest level, it spirals up through the house, at first deeply channeled between two walls, then made more open, becoming less safe as it eventually climbs to the fourth level. As it reaches the sky, the stair loses all connection with the safety of the ground.

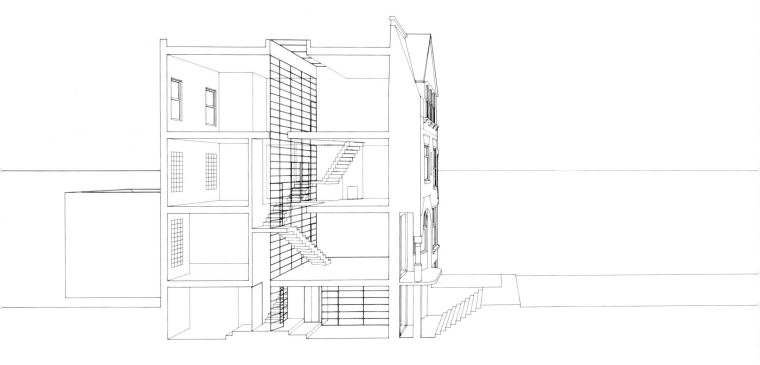

▲ *Section Perspective.*

An ordinary glass curtain wall is taken from the curbside and transplanted inside a home. The two facades coexist, like immigrants from different continents. The conventional brownstone town house is transformed into an event. Spiraling up through the different levels, the stair defies expectations, turning the ordinary process of commuting between floors into an increasingly dynamic experience. Each door leads from where you are to where you have been and back again. The relationship between the stone and glass faces is left open to interpretation. ■

▶ *Detached from the glass surface, the stair is an abstract object in the living room.*

LEAVING   PRESSURE   ROOTLESS   HISTORY IS OVER

appendix

Joe Valerio   Mark Dewalt   Jim Bogatto   Michael Everts

THE FIRMS

A number of people have worked with Joe Valerio over
the course of his 20 plus years of professional practice.
Photographed above is the current management team
of Valerio Dewalt Train Associates: the principals—
Joe Valerio and Mark Dewalt—and the associates—
Jim Bogatto, Michael Everts, David Jennerjahn,
Randy Mattheis, David Rasche, and Neil J. Sheehan.
A list of individuals, regrettably incomplete,
employed by Joe Valerio follows.

VALERIO DEWALT TRAIN ASSOCIATES, INC.

Chicago, Illinois

1994-1998

principals

Mark Dewalt
Gene Montgomery (retired)
Jack Train (retired)
Joe Valerio
Ken Wertz (retired)

associates

Jim Bogatto
Michael Everts
David Jennerjahn
Randy Mattheis
David Rasche
Neil J. Sheehan

professional staff

Jeff Berta
Michael Carline
Pamela S. Crowell
Mark Cuellar
Michael Cygan
Mary Delany
Ted Duncan
David Dylo
Zisong Feng
Kim Frutiger
Mark S. Fitzgerald
Kasia Gawlik Parker
Jason Hall
Daniel Harmon

Kurt Hunt
Daniel Ikeda
Ewa Jankiewicz-Hally
Elana Katz
Stephen Katz
Andrea Kiesling
Brian Korte
Brian Maite
Christine McGrath
Wendy Mingin
Michelle Molnar Schneider
Sarah Morie
Ericka Pagel
Brad Pausha
Viorica Pisau
Jeff Pivorunas
Louis Ray
Paul Reich
Jorge Reyes
Marius Ronnett
Heather Salisbury
Dana Sanchez
Gisela Schmidt
Rosa Shyn
Andrew To
Ban Tran
Heather Wasilowski
James Wild
Steve Wilmot

development directors

Peggy Adducci
Deborah Rashman Carpman

David Jennerjahn   Randy Mattheis   David Rasche   Neil J. Sheehan

interns

Joel Agacki

Anselmo Cannefora

Carlos Concepcion

Ken Chow

Matthew Crummey

Michael Flath

Tracey Jo Hoekstra

Rebecca Korson

David Perez

Mark Witte

VALERIO-ASSOCIATES, INC.

Chicago, Illinois

1988-1994

president

Joe Valerio

associates

David Jennerjahn

Randy Mattheis

professional staff

Barbara Arendt

Emily Britton

Michael Cygan

Michael Everts

Scott Georgeson

Dan Ikeda

Mark Klancic

Janice Ladouceur

Louis Lovera

Adrienne Osborne

Brad Pausha

Gregory Randall

Lilya Sirazi

Shawn Trentlage

Kurt Young Binter

interns

Brian Buchowski

Robert Chambers

Joe Cortez

Mark Demsky

Patrick McGuire

Adrienne Osborne

A. EPSTEIN AND SONS INTERNATIONAL, INC.

Chicago, Illinois

1986-1988

SWANKE HAYDEN CONNELL ARCHITECTS

Chicago, Illinois

1985-1986

CHRYSALIS CORP. ARCHITECTS

Milwaukee, Wisconsin

1970-85

principals

Joe Valerio

Kent Hubbell

professional staff

John Arlienne

Libby Barber

Holly Bieniewski

Mary Campbell

Gretchen Dahl

Todd Davies

Pamela Doucette

Mark Ernst

Daniel S. Friedman

Michael Garber

Henry Grabowski

Joseph Haupt

Rebecca James

Vince James

Wes Janz

David Jennerjahn

Chris Krouser

Joel Krueger

Randy Mattheis

Paul Mueller

Phoebe O'Brien

Beth Partleton

Gary Rebholz

Larry St. Germain

James Shields

Charlie Simonds

Lawrence Stern

Michael Szczawinski

Eric Tirrell

Tuan Tran

Nancy Willert

Bill Williams

Karen Wolfert

interns

Julie Deprey

Patricia Gill

Katherine Keane

Robert Musgnug

Chuck Riesterer

Chicago and the Midwest have served as Joe Valerio's home throughout his professional career. Born in 1947, he grew up in the Rogers Park neighborhood of Chicago and then Wilmette, a north shore suburb of Chicago. He first left Chicago to attend the University of Michigan, receiving a bachelor of architecture in 1970. This was followed with a two-year stay in Los Angeles, where he earned a Master of Architecture degree from UCLA.

In 1970 Joe Valerio began working with Chrysalis Corp. Architects, formed by Alan Stanton, Mike Davies, and Chris Dawson. The firm focused on interdisciplinary design approaches teaming architects, artists, and scientists. These explorations led to an interest in experimental structures, including tensile and pneumatic systems. During 1972 he directed the firm's effort to design an exhibition for the Smithsonian and the American Association for the Advancement of Science in Washington, D.C.

In 1973 he accepted a position at the recently formed University of Wisconsin—Milwaukee's School of Architecture and Urban Planning, becoming an associate professor. During the 1970s he founded C.O.W. (Chrysalis of Wisconsin), working with Kent Hubbell until 1981. From 1981 to 1985 he continued to develop his explorations, working on projects from coast to coast.

In 1985 it was time to return to Chicago. Joe joined Swanke Hayden Connell Architects as design director. At this time he also resigned his position at U.W.—Milwaukee. This transitional period marked two significant changes: returning home and working for someone else. In 1986 he moved to A. Epstein & Sons International, Inc., an architecture and engineering firm, as vice president of architecture. In early 1988 it became clear that there were thoughts and ideas which needed to be explored in architecture in Chicago. There was too much inertia in the older architectural organizations in the city to allow this to happen.

Valerio-Associates, Inc., was formed in 1988. Over the course of six years the firm grew to a staff of eight. Joe Valerio worked on a variety of projects, including residential, restaurants, retail, and manufacturing facilities, many receiving awards. Always an advocate of nurturing client relationships, Joe and his team worked on a small renovation of a manufacturing facility in Skokie, Illinois. The project developed into a six-year relationship with the client, U.S. Robotics Corporation, which has continued with its merger partner, 3Com Corporation.

1994 was the year that Valerio-Associates, Inc., merged with another Chicago firm, Train Dewalt Associates. The business and technical strengths of the latter were added to the design skills of the former, creating Valerio Dewalt Train Associates. As design principal, Joe Valerio has overseen many of the firm's projects, including a $30-million, mixed-use block redevelopment in downtown Madison, Wisconsin, which includes a new 10-story office building, a 537-car parking structure, a variety of renovations and expansions, and the development of new retail space. He has also overseen the planning and design of a $256-million Midwest regional research and office campus for 3Com Corporation (formally U.S. Robotics).

Concurrent with his professional practice, Joe Valerio has worked with a number of organizations, including the national and local chapters of the American Institute of Architects, the Chicago Architecture Club, the Contemporary Arts Council, Society of Contemporary Arts at the Art Institute of Chicago, and the Museum of Contemporary Art. He has served as a consultant to the National Endowment for the Arts, the National Academy of Sciences, and the American Association for the Advancement of Sciences.

A successful design begins with a good idea, develops into a successful client relationship, and is recognized by one's peers. This recognition includes four National AIA Honor Awards, nine Chicago Chapter AIA Honor Awards, and six Wisconsin Chapter AIA Awards. In addition, he has been recognized for design leadership by the Architectural League of New York in its "Emerging Voices" series. In 1986 he was selected by Philip Johnson and Robert Stern to participate in their "40 under 40" exhibition. In 1993 he became a fellow of the American Institute of Architects.

organizational service
President, Contemporary Arts Council of Chicago, Illinois, 1998
Chair, AIA Committee on Design, 1997
President, Chicago Architecture Club, 1994
Executive Board, Contemporary Arts Council of Chicago, Illinois, 1994
Executive Board, Men's Council, Museum of Contemporary Art, 1989-1991
Society for Contemporary Art, Art Institute of Chicago, 1985-1990
Design Committee Programs Chairman, AIA/Chicago Chapter, 1990
Long Range Planning Committee, AIA/Chicago Chapter, 1992

professional/academic positions
Principal, Valerio Dewalt Train Associates, Inc., 1994 to present
President, Valerio-Associates, Inc., 1988 to 1994
Vice President of Architecture, A. Epstein and Sons International, Inc., 1985 to 1986
Design Director, Swanke Hayden Connell Architects, 1986 to 1988
Associate Professor, University of Wisconsin—Milwaukee, 1973 to 1986
President, Chrysalis Corporation Architects, 1970 to 1985

consulting positions
USG Interiors
Formica Corporation
American Association for the Advancement of Sciences
National Academy of Sciences
National Endowment for the Arts

visiting critic and lecturer
University of Nebraska, 1998
Illinois Institute of Technology, 1998
Chicago Chapter AIA Lecture Series, 1996
AIA Lecture Series, Washington University of St. Louis, 1995
"Chicago From a New Perspective," AIA Chicago 125th Anniversary
Lecture Series, 1994
Chicago Athenaeum, 1994, 1996
Miami University of Ohio, 1994
Renaissance Society, University of Chicago, 1994
University of Illinois—Champaign, 1994
University of Illinois—Chicago, 1994
Washington University of St. Louis, 1993
University of Wisconsin—Milwaukee, 1986, 1990, 1993
UCLA, 1983, 1991
Arizona State University, 1981, 1983, 1987, 1991
University of Michigan, 1990
Madison Art Center, 1984
The Architectural League of New York, 1984
University of Arizona, 1983
University of Maryland, 1980

honors
Architectural Record Interiors, 1993, 1995, 1996
Chicago Chapter, AIA, Interiors Award, 1988, 1990, 1992,
1995 (2), 1996, 1997(2)
National AIA Honor Award, 1981, 1993
National AIA Honor Award for Interiors, 1993, 1996
Institute of Business Designers—Chicago, Distinguished Interior Award, 1993
Fellow, American Institute of Architects, 1993
Progressive Architecture, Design Award, 1991
Architectural Record Houses, 1983, 1991
Chicago Chapter, Distinguished Building Award(s), 1991(2), 1993
Institute of Business Designers, Gold Medal, 1988
Wisconsin Society of Architects Honor Awards, 1975, 1981, 1984, 1985
"Emerging Voices", *Interiors* Magazine, 1985
"Emerging Voices in Architecture," Architectural League of New York, 1984
Governor's Award for Design Excellence, State of Michigan, 1979

exhibitions
"Stairs and Elevators: The Ups and Downs of Architecture," The Art Institute of Chicago, 1998
"New Chicago Architecture," American Pavilion at Sao Paulo Bienal, The Chicago Athenaeum, 1997.
"Ingenious Solutions," Chicago Chapter AIA/Chicago Architecture Foundation, 1996
"The Chicago and Midwest Villa," The Chicago Athenaeum, 1996
"AIA Awards Exhibition," Chicago Historical Society, 1995, 1996
"New Chicago Interiors," The Chicago Athenaeum, 1995
The DIA Foundation, New York, 1994
"The Chicago Villa," The Chicago Athenaeum, 1994
"Turn of the Century Home," Renaissance Society, University of Chicago, 1994
"Dream Houses," Contemporary Arts Center, Cincinnati, Ohio, 1993
"Chicago Architecture," Chicago Historical Society, 1991, 1993
"Half Time," 75 Years of Chicago Architecture, Chicago Arts Club, 1992
West Hollywood City Center Competition, Exhibition, 1987
Chicago Architectural Club, Chicago, Illinois, 1986-1994
Formica Corporation, IDCNY, 1992
Eight Houses, Falling Water Development, Pacific-Sakata Corporation, 1991
"Rumors About the American House," Gwenda Jay Gallery, Chicago, 1991
"Found Futures," USG Design Center, 1992
Matteson Public Library Competition, Exhibition, 1990
"Forty Under Forty," an exhibition of the work for forty architects
selected by Philip Johnson and Robert A. M. Stern, 1986

WORKS ON JOE VALERIO

Arcidi, Philip. "Small Town as Urban Prosthesis." *Progressive Architecture* (November 1989): 28-30.

Bierman, M. Lindsay. "AIA Honor Awards: Celebrating Pluralism." *Architecture* 82, no. 5 (May 1993): 87-111.

Boles, Daralice D. "At Home in Arizona." *Progressive Architecture* (October 1985): 92-95.

Borys, Ann Marie. "Cincinnati Exhibit of Dream Houses." *Architecture* 83, no. 1 (January 1994): 27-31.

Brenner, Douglas. "Architecture Goes Soft." *Horizon: The Cultural Scene* (October 1978) (reprint form October 1978 Issue of Horizon Magazine.). Pub. No. 12-FS-9401.

Broto, Carles. "Valerio Dewalt Train: Gardner Residence (Chicago, Illinois) 1993." *Domestic Interiors* (Barcelona: Monsa de Ediciones, 1997), 124-133.

Davies, Michael J. P. "Dynamic Structures: Case Studies." *Building Research: Journal of the BRAB Building Research Institute. Air Structures* 9, no. 1. Benjamin H. Evans, AIA editor (January/March 1972): 37-38.

"Design Awards/Competitions." *Architectural Record* 177, no. 12 (October 1989): 64-65.

Dixon, John Morris. "The Santa Monica School: What's Its Lasting Contribution?" *Progressive Architecture* (May 1995): 63-71.

Futagawa, Yukio, publisher/editor. "Joseph Valerio: Gardner Residence." *Global Architecture Houses* 50 (October 1996): 80-87.

Futagawa, Yukio, editor/publisher. "Joseph Valerio: Cincinnati Dream House. Suburban U.S.A. Design: 1993" *Global Architecture Houses* 48 (March, 1996): 122-123.

Gatland, Laura. "Industrious Designs Set Companies Apart." *Focus: Architecture* Chicago (November 1997): 17, 19.

Geiger, David H, Ph. D. "Pneumatic Structures." *Progressive Architecture* LIII, no. 7 (August 1972): 81-89.

Goldstein, Barbara. "News Report: New Signs at the Salon du Meuble." *Progressive Architecture* (March 1985): 32.

Goldstein, Barbara. "Adventurous Taste: European Furniture Trends." *Arts + Architecture* 4, no. 2 (July 1985): 17-18.

Hartung, Martin. "Modernisme på mode: after et par årtiers skyggetilværelse er den modernistiske arkitektur nu igen ved at Komme til ære og værdighed I USA." *Berlingske Tidende*, Sektion 4, p. 3.

Jack, Michael. "1993 Interior Awards: Diverse View of Excellence." Memo: The Review of People, Information and Ideas. *The American Institute of Architects Newsletter* (September 1993): 11.

Kingsley, Charles. "World: Chrysalis Structures." *The Architectural Review* CLXIV, no. 977 (July 1978): 9.

Kolasinski, Annette, ed. "Chicago Firms Out in Front in 1993." *Focus: AIA Chicago* (February 1993): 5-8.

Krohe, James Jr. "Suburban Rumors: The Gang of Eight Comes to Burr Ridge, Illinois." *Inland Architecture* 36, no. 1 (January/February, 1992): 50-55.

Laine, Christian K., Editor. "Colton Senior Housing." *Metropolitan Review of Architecture, Art, Design, Urban Planning, Interiors, Culture, Theory, History, the City and the House* vol. II, no. 3 (May/June 1989): 62-65.

Lautman, Victoria. "Under the Golden Arches: Valerio Associates' Interior Renovation Links a Building's Structuralist Past With a View to the Future." *Architectural Record: Record Interiors* 181, no. 9 (September 1993): 84-89.

Lewin, Susan Grant. "A Romantic Past and a Dazzling Future." *House Beautiful* 124, no. 4 (April 1982): 108-111.

Lewis, Roger K. "18 Diverse Projects Awarded AIA's Annual Design Honors." *The Washington Post*, (30 January 1993): D1, D7.

Linn, Charles. "Modulating in Industrial Space." *Architectural Record: Record Interiors* review of UWest (September 1996): 98-101.

"Living: Lighting the Darkened Palaces." *Time* 115, no. 18 (5 May 1980): 82-83.

Mays, Vernon. "AIA Honor Awards: Interiors," review of Gardner Residence. *Architecture* 85, no. 6 (May 1996): 209.

McKee, Bradford. "AIA Announces Interior Architecture Awards." *Architecture* 83, no. 6 (June 1993): 23.

McNair, Andrew. "Forty Under Forty." *Interiors* (September 1986): 149-194.

Minke, Gernot. "Structures Membranes: Nouvelles Solutions Constructives, Nouvelles Possibilités d'Application." *techniques & ARCHITECTURE* 304 (May/June 1975): 85-101.

Murphy, Jim. "A Light Language: The Work of Chrysalis East, Milwaukee." *Progressive Architecture* vol.LVIII, no. 2 (February 1977): 64-71.

Nakamura, Toshio, ed. "New Work: Three Rivers Events Structure / Summerfest Main Stage / Performance Enclosure for the Ann Arbor Street Fair / Structures for the Lakefront Festival of the Arts / Pabst Stage / Sportshaven an Athletic Training Center / Humboldt Park Bandshell / Herman Miller Enclosure / Dixie Mall Shopping Center / MATC Agribusiness Enclosure by Chrysalis East." *Architecture + Urbanism*, no. 91 (May, 1978): 63-74.

Nathan, Scott A. "Valerio Designs for Seniors." *Inland Architect* 33 no. 5 (September/October 1989): 17, 21.

Nelson, George. "Tents: A 'Feast for the Senses,' Tents can Provide Interior Spaces in which People Thrive." *Interiors* CXXXVIII, no. 5 (December 1978): 72-75.

Nereim, Anders. "Exercising Options." *Architectural Record* 179, no. 1 (January, 1991): 84-87.

Nereim, Andres. "Valerio Associates." *Inland Architect* 33, no. 2 (March/April 1989): 36-37.

Nesmith, Lynn. "News: Chicago Eight Design Model Houses." *Architecture* 80, no. 12 (December 1991): 25.

Pearson, Clifford. "Turning the Corner." *Architectural Record: Houses* 179, no. 4 (April 1991): 92-97.

Schmertz, Mildred F., exec. editor. "Reinhard House." *Architectural Record: Record Houses* (Mid-May 1983): 94-97.

Stein, Karen D. "Breaking the Mold: Nearly 60 Floors in the Air, Joe Valerio has Created an Idealized World of Metal and Wood." *Architectural Record* 183, no. 9 (September 1995): 104-109.

Stein, Karen D. "Energy Field," review of Ustate Office and Research Center. *Architectural Record* 183, no. 2 (February 1995): 98-101.

Wagner, Michael. "Emerging Voices: Joseph Valerio" *Interiors* (September 1985): 164-169.

Zevon, Susan. "Joseph Valerio: Creating a Cultural Marker" in *Inside Architecture: Interiors by Architects* (London: Thames and Hudson, 1996), 40-47.

"Architectural Design Citation: Colton Palms." *Progressive Architecture* LXXII, no. 1 (January 1991): 102-103.

The Architect's Dream: Houses for the Next Millennium. Exhibit curated by Daniel S. Friedman, AIA. 19 November 1993 - 23 January 1994. Cincinnati, Ohio: The Contemporary Arts Center Cincinnati, 1993.

"Colton Palms Apartments in Colton, California." *Architektur + Wettbewerbe* 153 (March 1993): 3-4.

"Interiors Platform." *Interiors* (October 1987): 20, 24.

"Members' Voices: Where do you get your Design Inspiration?" *AIA Architect* 4 (July 1997): 8.

"New Visions for Old Age," *Architecture* 83, no. 10 (October 1994): 88.

"News Report: Megastructure Community Wins Reynolds Student Prize."
Progressive Architecture vol. LII, no. 5 (May 1971): 34.

"Outlook: Two Arkansas Students Win Reynolds Prize with 'Provocative'
Concept." *AIA Journal* 55, no. 5 (May 1971): 8.

"PIA News: Housing PIA Explores 'Universal Truths'." *AIA Architect*, vol. 3
(February 1996): 12.

"Projects" review of Beans and Barley Cafe. *Wisconsin Architect*. AIA Wisconsin,
(March/April 1995): 12.

"Réalisations du Grupe Chrysalis," *techniques + ARCHITECTURE*, no. 304,
(Mai-June 1975): 96-97.

"T.V. Studio is 'Craned' Into Place." *Architectural Record* (October 1996): 17.

"Tensistrutture e Gonfiabili." (Structures built for multiple purposes)
Domus no. 569 (April 1977): 45.

WORKS BY JOE VALERIO

Valerio, Joseph M., ed. *Architectural Fabric Structures: The Use of Tensioned
Fabric Structures by Federal Agencies*, by the National Research Council (U.S.);
Advisory Board on the Built Environment; Commission on Engineering and
Technical Systems; and National Research Council. Washington, D.C.: National
Academy Press, 1985.

Valerio, Joseph. "Architectural Object: Versus Space." *Domus* no. 642
(September 1983): 32-37.

Valerio, Joseph. "Herz Residence." *Architecture + Urbanism*, no. 156
(September 1983): 68-72.

Valerio, Joseph. "Innocent Buildings: A Critique of Historical Form."
Inland Architect 36, no. 2 (March/April, 1992): 62-64.

Valerio, Joseph. "Reinhard Residence." *Architecture + Urbanism* no. 156
(September 1983): 73-77.

Valerio, Joseph M., Michael Davies, and Alan Stanton. "Air Structures:
Inflatable Alternatives." *Saturday Review: Science* LV, no. 52. (23 December
1972): 23-32.

Valerio, Joseph M. and Daniel Friedman. *Movie Palaces: Renaissance and
Reuse*. Edited by Nancy Morison Ambler. New York, NY: Educational Facilities
Laboratories Division, Academy for Educational Development, 1982.

Valerio, Joseph and Kent Hubbell. "Chrysalis East: Project for Hershman
Residence, Chicago Illinois, USA." *Architecture + Urbanism: Contemporary
Houses of the World*, no. 101 (February 1979): 7-10, 19-22.

Valerio, Joseph and Kent Hubbell. "Structures Légères aux U.S.A." *techniques
& ARCHITECTURE* no. 333 (December 1980): 103-107.

Valerio, Joseph M. with Randall Mattheis and David Jennerjahn. "Three Works
by Joseph Valerio," review of Coosa Pines Health Center, Colton Palms, Ohio
House. *Architecture + Urbanism* 266 (November 1992): 34-53.

Valerio, Joseph, Alan Stanton, and Michael Davies. "Air Structures" in *Amerika*
vol. 202 (April 1973), 23-24.

Valerio, Joe and Thomas Vonier. "Capital City Readout—AAAS Communications
Experiment: A Regional Information Exchange on the Employment of Science
and Technology in Relation to the Needs of the Washington, D.C., Area."
Science 178, no. 4060 (3 November 1972): 526.

CITATIONS

unexpected

[1] Daniel J. Boorstin, *The Americans: The Colonial Experience*.
(New York: Random House, 1958), 151.

[2] Daniel J. Boorstin, *The Americans: The Colonial Experience*.
(New York: Random House, 1958), 158.

leaving

[1] Louis H. Sullivan, from *Kindergarten Chats (revised 1918) and Other Writings*.
(New York: George Wittenborn, Inc., 1947), 44.

[2] Adolf Loos, "Ornament and Crime" in *Programs and Manifestoes on 20th-
Century Architecture*. ed. by Ulrich Conrads. Translated by Michael Bullock.
(Cambridge, Massachusetts: The MIT Press, 1989), 24.

[3] Herbert Muschamp, "The American Lawn: Surface of Everyday Life" in the Arts
and Leisure Section of *The New York Times* (Sunday, July 5, 1998), 1 and 32.

pressure

[1] Michael Sorkin. "The Real Thing" in *Exquisite Corpse: Writing on Buildings*.
(London: Verso, 1994), 173.

rootless

[1] Daniel J. Boorstin, *The Americans: The Colonial Experience*.
(New York: Random House, 1958), 150.

[2] Adolf Loos, "Ornament and Crime" in *Programs and Manifestoes on 20th-
Century Architecture*. ed. by Ulrich Conrads. Translated by Michael Bullock.
(Cambridge, Massachusetts: The MIT Press, 1989), 20.

[3] Adolf Loos, "Ornament and Crime" in *Programs and Manifestoes on 20th-
Century Architecture*. ed. by Ulrich Conrads. Translated by Michael Bullock.
(Cambridge, Massachusetts: The MIT Press, 1989), 20.

[4] Thomas Jefferson, "Books for a Statesman: To James Madison" in *Writings*, ed.
by Merrill D. Peterson. (New York: Literary Classics of the United States, Inc.:
1984), 822.

[5] Joan Ockman, "Pneumotopian Visions" in *Metropolis* 17, no. 9 (June 1998),
118.

history is over

[1] Vincent Scully, *American Architecture and Urbanism*, new rev. ed. (New York:
Henry Holt & Company, 1988), 12-13.

innocence

[1] Garry Wills, "Two Sides of Innocence," *Time: The Weekly Magazine* (July 14,
1997), 71.

[2] Robert Venturi, Denise Scott Brown, Steven Izeneur, *Learning From Las Vegas:
The Forgotten Symbolism of Architectural Form*, 12th printing, 1993
(Cambridge, Massachusetts: MIT Press, 1977), 148.

self-evidence

[1] Daniel J. Boorstin, *The Americans: The Colonial Experience*.
(New York: Random House, 1958), 151-152.

ambiguity

[1] *The Random House College Dictionary*.

CHRYSALIS CORP. ARCHITECTURE

1973

p r o j e c t : **Three Rivers Festival Eventstructure** ◀
c l i e n t : Three Rivers Arts Festival of the Carnegie Institute
s i t e : Pittsburgh, Pennsylvania
c o m p l e t e d : 1975
t e a m : Joe Valerio, Kent Hubbell, Michael Szczawinski, Aerovironment, Inc. (aeronautical engineering), Walter R. Ratai, Inc. (m/e/p engineering)
a w a r d s : 1977 Wisconsin Society of Architects Award
p h o t o s : Joe Valerio

1974

p r o j e c t : **Summerfest Main Stage Tensile Structure**
c l i e n t : Milwaukee World Festival Inc.
s i t e : Henry Maier Festival Grounds; Milwaukee, Wisconsin

p r o j e c t : **Structure for Year Round Horticultural Studies**
(Agribusiness Enclosure)
c l i e n t : Milwaukee Area Technical College
s i t e : Mequon, Wisconsin
c o m p l e t e d : 1976

1975

p r o j e c t : **Inside/Outside Inflatable Tradeshow Structure**
c l i e n t : Alcoa—Aluminum Company of America
s i t e : Pittsburgh, Pennsylvania
c o m p l e t e d : 1976

p r o j e c t : **Dixie Square Mall Renovation**
c l i e n t : M & J Wilkow Ltd. Partnership
s i t e : Harvey, Illinois

1976

p r o p o s a l : **Humboldt Park Bandshell**
c l i e n t : Milwaukee County Park Commission
s i t e : Milwaukee, Wisconsin

p r o p o s a l : **A National Terratectural Competition**
for a Capitol Building Annex
c l i e n t : The State of Minnesota
s i t e : Minneapolis, Minnesota
t e a m : Joe Valerio with Kahler, Slater and Fitzhugh Scott, Inc.

1977

p r o j e c t : **Tensile Structures for the Lakefront Festival of the Arts**
c l i e n t : Friends of Art, Milwaukee Art Museum
s i t e : Milwaukee, Wisconsin

p r o j e c t : **Milwaukee Conservatory: Mitchell Park Dome Tension Structure**
c l i e n t : Milwaukee County Park System
s i t e : Milwaukee, Wisconsin

p r o j e c t : **Pabst Performance Stage**
c l i e n t : Milwaukee World Festival, Inc.
s i t e : Henry Maier Festival Grounds; Milwaukee, Wisconsin

1978

p r o j e c t : **Alewives Stage**
c l i e n t : Milwaukee Performing Arts Center
s i t e : Milwaukee, Wisconsin
c o m p l e t e d : Milwaukee, Wisconsin

p r o j e c t : **ChicagoFest Entry Structure**
c l i e n t : Festivals, Inc.
s i t e : Chicago, Illinois

p r o j e c t : **Survival Structure**
c l i e n t : School of Architecture and Urban Planning,
University of Wisconsin—Milwaukee
s i t e : Point Beach State Park in Two Rivers, Wisconsin

1979

p r o j e c t : **Alewives Concession Stand**
c l i e n t : Milwaukee Performing Arts Center
s i t e : Milwaukee, Wisconsin
c o m p l e t e d : 1979

p r o j e c t : **Hershman / Reinhard House** ◀
c l i e n t : Seymour and Shirley Hershman / Keith and Rose Lee Reinhard
s i t e : Chicago, Illinois
c o m p l e t e d : 1980
t e a m : Joe Valerio (partner-in-charge), Kent Hubbell, Henry Grabowski, Mark Ernst, Marg Davis (interiors), Anthony Schnarsky (structural engineering), Stanley Construction (general contractor).
a w a r d s : 1981 AIA Honor Award; 1983 *Architectural Record*, Record Houses Award
p h o t o s : Barbara Karant of Karant + Associates, Inc. and Joe Valerio

p r o j e c t : **Medlar Cottage**
c l i e n t : Robert and Alice Medlar
s i t e : Dexter, Michigan

1980

p r o j e c t : **Baltimore Bridges: Inner Harbor Development Project** ◀
c l i e n t : Inner Harbor Development Project
s i t e : Baltimore, Maryland
c o m p l e t e d : 1981
t e a m : Kent Hubbell (partner-in-charge), Joe Valerio, Dan Dennison, Michael Bruner, Steven Nash, Robert Darvas Associates (structural engineering)
p h o t o s : Joe Valerio and Kent Hubbell

p r o j e c t : **ChicagoFest Graphics Program**
c l i e n t : Festivals, Inc.
s i t e : Chicago, Illinois

p r o j e c t : **The Herz Residence**
c l i e n t : Thomas and Maxine Herz
s i t e : Shorewood, Wisconsin
c o m p l e t e d : 1982
a w a r d : 1984 Wisconsin Society of Architects Award

1981

p r o p o s a l : **South Entry for the Grand Avenue** ◀
c l i e n t : Milwaukee Redevelopment Corporation
s i t e : Milwaukee, Wisconsin
p h o t o s : Joe Valerio

1983

p r o j e c t : **Arbour Park Apartments** ◀
c l i e n t : Richard Marmor, Arbour Development Company
s i t e : Tempe, Arizona
c o m p l e t e d : 1985
t e a m : Joe Valerio (partner-in-charge), Vincent James, John Arlienne
p h o t o s : Barbara Karant of Karant + Associates, Inc.

p r o j e c t : **Blandin Credit Union**
c l i e n t : Blandin Paper Company
s i t e : Grand Rapids, Minnesota
c o m p l e t e d : 1985

p r o j e c t : **C.U.N.A. Credit Union**
c l i e n t : C.U.N.A. Credit Union
s i t e : Madison, Wisconsin
c o m p l e t e d : 1985
a w a r d s : 1985 Wisconsin Society of Architects Award

p r o j e c t : **The Griffith House** ◀
c l i e n t : Gary and Carol Griffith
s i t e : Hubertus, Wisconsin
c o m p l e t e d : 1984
t e a m : Joe Valerio (partner-in-charge), Vincent James
a w a r d s : 1984 Wisconsin Society of Architects Award
p h o t o s : Larry W. Schwarm

SELECTED WORK

a chronology of
buildings and projects
listed by
year of design

◀ indicates that
the project is presented
in this book.

project: **Kilbourn Row Townhouses**
client: City Lights Development, Inc.
site: Milwaukee, Wisconsin
completed: 1984, Phase One; 1985, Phase Two
awards: 1984 Wisconsin Society of Architects Awards

project: **Renville Farmers Co-op Credit Union**
client: Renville Farmers Co-op Credit Union
site: Renville, Minnesota
completed: 1984

project: **Teachers Federation Credit Union** ◄
client: Teachers Federation Credit Union
site: Minneapolis, Minnesota
completed: 1985
team: Joe Valerio (partner-in-charge), Randy Mattheis, David Jennerjahn, Michael Garber, Nancy Willert (interiors consultant), Amman and Whitney (structural engineering), D.J. Kranz (general contractor)
photos: Vincent James

1 9 8 4
project: **Bowman House Renovations**
client: Russell and Barbara Bowman
site: Milwaukee, Wisconsin

project: **Dragos House**
client: Stephen F. Dragos
site: Bayside, Wisconsin
completed: 1984
award: 1984 Wisconsin Society of Architects Honor Award

project: **Gaetano's Restaurant**
client: The Rouse Company and Thomas LoCoco
site: Grand Avenue Shopping Mall in Milwaukee, Wisconsin
completed: 1985

project: **Hennepin Center Offices for CCCU**
client: City County Credit Union
site: Minneapolis, Minnesota
completed: 1985

project: **Maquoketa State Bank Renovation**
client: Maquoketa State Bank
site: Maquoketa, Iowa
completed: 1985

project: **Qureshi Cottage**
client: Dr. Ijaz and Mrs. Georgene Qureshi
site: Sister Bay, Wisconsin
completed: 1987

project: **Schlitz Brewery Redevelopment Master Plan**
client: Brewery Works, Inc., a subsidiary of Grunau Development Company
site: Milwaukee, Wisconsin

S W A N K E   H A Y D E N
C O N N E L L   A R C H I T E C T S
1 9 8 5
proposal: **Church of Religious Science** ◄
client: Church of Religious Science, Chicago
team: Neil Frankel (principal), Joe Valerio (design director), David Jennerjahn
site: Chicago, Illinois
photos: David Jennerjahn

project: **Manufacturers Hanover Trust**
client: Manufacturers Hanover Trust Co.
site: Chicago, Illinois
completed: 1986

proposal: **Marina City Office Tower**
client: Marina City Partnership, Inc.
site: Napervile, Illinois

1 9 8 6
proposal: **Microdynamics**
client: Microdynamics, Inc.
site: Naperville, Illinois

A .   E P S T E I N   A N D   S O N S ,
I N T E R N A T I O N A L   I N C .
1 9 8 6
proposal: **Pillsbury Research and Development Headquarters** ◄
client: Pillsbury Corporation
site: Minneapolis, Minnesota
team: Joe Valerio (principal designer), Jim Stefanski (project manager), Randy Mattheis, Lawrence Stern
photos: Randy Mattheis and Joe Valerio

project: **1122 Clark Street Apartments**
client: Clark Street Partners
site: Chicago, Illinois
completed: 1988

proposal/project: **North Point Marina Administration Building**
client: North Point Marina
site: Waukegan, Illinois
completed: 1986 proposal presented; 1989 revised design built

V A L E R I O - A S S O C I A T E S ,   I N C .
1 9 8 7
project: **The Oriental Theater**
client: Paramount Theatre Corporation
site: Milwaukee, Wisconsin
completed: 1988
awards: 1990 AIA Chicago, Honor Award for Interior Architecture

1 9 8 8
project: **Coosa Pines Health Center** ◄
client: Kimberly-Clark Corporation
site: Coosa Pines, Alabama
completed: 1990
team: Joe Valerio (principal-in-charge), Randy Mattheis (project architect), David Jennerjahn, Gregory Randall, Brad Pausha, Daniel Ikeda, Nancy Willert (interior consultant), EWI Engineering Associates (civil engineering), A. Epstein and Sons International, Inc. (structural, mechanical and electrical engineering), Universal Construction Company, a division of Turner Construction (general contractors)
awards: 1991 AIA Chicago, Certificate of Merit, Distinguished Building Award
photos: Barbara Karant of Karant + Associates, Inc.

project: **Colton Palms Apartments** ◄
client: Cooperative Services, Inc. and the City of Colton Redevelopment Agency
site: Colton, California
completed: 1991
team: Joe Valerio (principal-in-charge), David Jennerjahn (project architect), Randy Mattheis, Mark Klancic, Brad Pausha, Daniel Ikeda, Nancy Willert (interiors consultant), Robert Darvas Associates (structural engineers), WMA Consulting Engineers, Ltd. (mechanical and electrical engineering), EWI Engineering Associates, Inc. (civil engineering), Midori Landscape (landscape architects), Turner Construction Company (general contractor)
awards: 1988 winner first stage of Colton Senior Housing Competition; 1989 winner second stage of Colton Senior Housing Competition, commission awarded; 1991 Progressive Architecture Award Citation, 1993 AIA Chicago Honor Award, Distinguished Building, 1993 AIA National Honor Award
photos: Barbara Karant of Karant + Associates, Inc., Joe Valerio, and Orlando Cabanban Photography (model shots)

project: **Leonards Metals Manufacturing and Office Facilities**
client: LMI Aerospace, Inc.

s i t e s : St. Charles, Missouri and Tulsa, Oklahoma
c o m p l e t e d : 1988 LMI Real Estate Master Plan; 1989 Mueller Road
Manufacturing Plan; 1997 Mueller Road Corporate Offices; 1994 Tulsa Metal
Treatment Facility; 1993 Highway 94 Drop Hammer Center.

1 9 8 9
p r o j e c t : **Ohio House** ◄
c l i e n t : Joe Valerio and Linda Searl
s i t e : Chicago, Illinois
c o m p l e t e d : 1989
t e a m : Joe Valerio and Linda Searl, Stearn-Joglekar (structural engineering),
WMA Consulting Engineers Ltd. (mechanical and electrical engineering),
Richard Van Pelt (general contractor)
a w a r d s : 1991 AIA Chicago Distinguished Building Honor Award,
1991 *Architectural Record*, Record Houses Award
p h o t o s : Barbara Karant of Karant + Associates, Inc.

1 9 9 1
p r o p o s a l : **In-Between House** (prototype) ◄
c l i e n t : Seiji Suzuki of Pacific-Sakata Development, Inc.
s i t e : Burr Ridge, Illinois
t e a m : Joe Valerio (principal-in-charge), Randy Mattheis, and
David Jennerjahn
p h o t o s : James Steinkamp of Steinkamp/Ballogg Chicago

p r o j e c t : **Essex Senior Apartments**
c l i e n t : Cooperative Services, Inc.
s i t e : Essex, Maryland
c o m p l e t e d : 1993

p r o j e c t : **The Can Addition—Warehouse and Raw Can Off Loading Facility**
c l i e n t : Pepsi Cola General Bottlers
s i t e : Chicago, Illinois

1 9 9 2
p r o j e c t : **U2 Manufacturing Facility** ◄
c l i e n t : U.S. Robotics Corporation
s i t e : Skokie, Illinois
c o m p l e t e d : 1992
t e a m : Joe Valerio (principal-in-charge), David Jennerjahn (project architect), Michael Cygan, Randy Mattheis, WMA Consulting Engineers Ltd. (m/e/p
engineering), Stearn/Joglekar, Ltd. (structural engineering), Nancy Willert
(interiors consultant), Turner Construction SPD (general contractor)
a w a r d s : 1993 Chicago Lighting Institute Award of Merit, 1993 Architectural
Record, Record Interiors Award, 1993 Chicago Athenaeum and Chicago IBD
Distinguished Interior, 1993 AIA National Interior Architecture Award of
Excellence, 1995 AIA Chicago Honor Award
p h o t o s : Barbara Karant of Karant + Associates, Inc.

p r o j e c t : **Gardner Apartment** ◄
c l i e n t : Tracy Gardner
s i t e : Chicago, Illinois
c o m p l e t e d : 1994
t e a m : Joe Valerio (principal-in-charge), Randy Mattheis (project architect),
Michael Cygan, Shawn Trentlage, Sarah Morie, Nancy Willert (interiors
consultant), Robert Darvas Associates (structural engineers), WMA Consulting
Engineers, Ltd. (m/e/p engineering), Turner Construction SPD (general
contractor)
a w a r d s : 1995 AIA Chicago Honor Award, Interior Architecture; 1995
Architectural Record Record Interiors Award; 1996 AIA National Honor
Award for Interiors
p h o t o s : Barbara Karant of Karant + Associates, Inc.

1 9 9 3
p r o j e c t : **Beans and Barley Market and Cafe** ◄
c l i e n t : 2B REAL LLC
s i t e : Milwaukee, Wisconsin
c o m p l e t e d : 1994
t e a m : from office of Valerio Dewalt Georgeson in Milwaukee, Wisconsin are
Scott Georgeson (partner-in-charge), Joe Valerio (design partner), Michael
Everts (project manager/designer), Nancy Willert (project designer), Brian
O'Looney, Ambrose Engineering (structural engineering), WMA Consulting
Engineers, Ltd. (m/e/p engineering), D.G. Beyer, Inc. (general contractor)
p h o t o s : Barbara Karant of Karant + Associates, Inc. and Ed Purcell

p r o p o s a l : **Dream House: The Enigma of the Rooms** ◄
e x h i b i t i o n : The Architect's Dream: Houses for the Next Millennium
c l i e n t : The Contemporary Arts Center
s i t e : Cincinnati, Ohio
c o m p l e t e d : 1993
t e a m : Joe Valerio (principal-in-charge), Randy Mattheis,
David Jennerjahn, Michael Cygan
p h o t o s : Barbara Karant, Karant + Associates, Inc. and
Orlando Cabanban Photography

p r o j e c t : **Warehouse Addition**
c l i e n t : Pepsi Cola General Bottlers
s i t e : Kansas City, Missouri

p r o j e c t : **U1 Office Building—Various Renovation Projects**
c l i e n t : U.S.Robotics Corporation
s i t e : Skokie, Illinois
c o m p l e t e d : 1995

p r o p o s a l : **U3 Manufacturing Center**
c l i e n t : U.S.Robotics Corporation
s i t e : Skokie, Illinois

p r o j e c t : **USG Solutions Center Product Sets**
c l i e n t : USG Corporation
s i t e : Chicago, Illinois
v a r i o u s : 1992 The Demented Laurentian Library (compasso);
1994 Look-Up brochure, 1994 Quadra/Cadre shots; 1995 Curvatura Theater
lobby; 1995 15 rooms sets including the Ring Shot; 1996 6 rooms Climaplus
including clean room shot; 1998 curved drywall ceiling system, 1998
Merchandise Mart Neocon installation; and 1998 stucco finish system.

p r o j e c t : **Ustate Office and Research Center** ◄
c l i e n t : U.S. Robotics Corporation
s i t e : Skokie, Illinois
c o m p l e t e d : 1993
t e a m : Joe Valerio (principal-in-charge), David Jennerjahn (project architect), Randy Mattheis, Michael Cygan, Louis Lovera, Mark Demsky, Nancy Willert
(interiors consultant), WMA Consulting Engineers, Ltd. (m/e/p engineering),
Turner Construction SPD (general contractor)
a w a r d s : 1995 Chicago Athenaeum Distinguished Interior Award
p h o t o s : Barbara Karant of Karant + Associates, Inc.

1 9 9 4
p r o p o s a l : **Sinai Temple** ◄
c l i e n t : Sinai Congregation
s i t e : Chicago, Illinois
t e a m : Joe Valerio and Linda Searl of Searl & Associates, P.C. (principals-in-
charge), Randy Mattheis, David Jennerjahn and from Searl & Associates, P.C.:
William Brockschmidt and Cynthia Dehoyos
p h o t o s : Barbara Karant, Karant + Associates, Inc.

p r o j e c t : **Tea Brew Facility**
c l i e n t : Pepsi Cola General Bottlers
s i t e : Munster, Indiana

**V A L E R I O   D E W A L T
T R A I N   A S S O C I A T E S ,   I N C .**

1 9 9 4
p r o j e c t : **UWest Manufacturing Center** ◄
c l i e n t : U.S. Robotics Corporation
s i t e : Morton Grove, Illinois
c o m p l e t e d : 1994
t e a m : Joe Valerio (principal-in-charge), David Jennerjahn (project architect), Jeff Berta, Daniel Harmon, Sarah Morie, Neil J. Sheehan, Nancy Willert
(interiors consultant), Peter Lindsay Schaudt (landscape architect), WMA
Consulting Engineers, Ltd. (m/e/p engineering), SDI Consultants, Ltd. (civil
engineering), Don Belford Associates (structural engineering), Turner
Construction Company (general contractor)
a w a r d s : 1996 AIA Chicago Honor Award for Interior Architecture, 1996
Record Interiors Award from *Architectural Record*
p h o t o s : Barbara Karant of Karant + Associates, Inc.

p r o j e c t : **Block 89 Multiuse Development◄**
c l i e n t : Urban Land Interests
s i t e : Madison, Wisconsin
c o m p l e t e d : 1999 (projected)
t e a m : Joe Valerio (principal-in-charge), David Jennerjahn (project architect), Jim Bogatto, Steve Wilmot, Elana Katz, Ted Duncan, James Wild, Heather Wasilowksi, Andrea Kiesling, Stephen Katz, Gisela Schmidt, Viorica Pisau, Tracy Hoekstra, Nancy Willert (interiors consultant), Robert Darvas Associates (structural engineers), Carl Walker, Inc. (parking consultant), Charter-Sills & Associates (lighting consultants), JJR, Inc. (civil and landscape), Woodward-Clyde Consultants (geotechnical), J.H. Findorff & Son, Inc. of Madison, Wisconsin (general contractor)
p h o t o s : Joe De Maio of De Maio Photography

p r o j e c t : **The Opera House Restaurant in Block 89 ◄**
c l i e n t : Chardonnezmoi, Inc.
s i t e : Madison, Wisconsin
c o m p l e t e d : 1996
t e a m : Joe Valerio (principal-in-charge), David Jennerjahn (project architect), Elana Katz, Jim Bogatto, Steve Wilmot, Andrea Kiesling, Nancy Willert (interiors consultant), Charter-Sills & Associates (exterior lighting consultant), Superior Lighting (interior lighting consultant), J.H. Findorff & Son, Inc. (general contractor)
p h o t o s : Joe De Maio of De Maio Photography

p r o j e c t : **Master Plan for Visitor Services at the Lincoln Park Zoo**
c l i e n t : Lincoln Park Zoological Society
s i t e : Chicago, Illinois

p r o j e c t : **Unet Manufacturing Facility ◄**
c l i e n t : U.S. Robotics Corporation and 3Com Corporation
s i t e : Mount Prospect, Illinois
c o m p l e t e d : 1999 (projected)
t e a m : Joe Valerio (principal-in-charge), Randy Mattheis (project architect), Ken Wertz, Daniel Ikeda, Michelle Molnar, Rosa Shyn, Mary Delany, Zisong Feng, Paul Reich, Ban Tran, Andrew To, Marius Ronnett, Neil J. Sheehan, Gisela Schmidt, Brad Pausha, Dana Sanchez, Michael Everts, Kurt Hunt, Michael Flath, Nancy Willert (interiors consultant), WMA Consulting Engineers, Ltd. (m/e/p engineering), SDI Consultants, Inc. (civil engineers), Gaiatech (environmental engineering), Charter-Sills & Associates (lighting consultants), Shiner + Associates (acoustical consultants), Peter Lindsay Schaudt, L.A. (landscape architects), Turner Construction (general contractor)
p h o t o s : Barbara Karant of Karant + Associates, Inc.

p r o j e c t : **Hawthorne Lane Restaurant**
c l i e n t : David and Annie Gingrass
s i t e : San Francisco, California

p r o j e c t : **Karant House**
c l i e n t : Barbara Karant
s i t e : Chicago, Illinois
c o m p l e t e d : 1999 (projected)

p r o j e c t : **Modular Factory for the Mobile Communications Division ◄**
c l i e n t : U.S. Robotics Corporation
s i t e : Salt Lake City, Utah
c o m p l e t e d : 1997
t e a m : collaboration with MHTN Architects of Salt Lake City, Utah (responsibilities included shell and core, landscape and architect of record), Joe Valerio (principal-in-charge), Michael Everts (project architect), Kasia Gawlik Parker, Ericka Pagel, Jason Hall, Viorica Pisau, Nancy Willert (interiors consultant), WMA Consulting Engineers (m/e/p engineering), Cini-Little International (food service consultants), Agra Engineering (soils engineering), Great Basin Engineering (civil engineering), Reaveley Engineers & Associates, Inc. (structural engineering), Bodell Construction (general contractor), Shiner + Associates (acoustic consultants)
p h o t o s : Barbara Karant of Karant + Associates, Inc. and Alan Blakely of Alan Blakely Photography

p r o p o s a l : **World Savings and Loan**
c l i e n t : World Savings and Loan
s i t e : Evanston, Illinois

p r o j e c t : **Turtle Wax Auto Appearance and Oil Change Facility**
c l i e n t : Turtle Wax Auto Appearance Centers, LLC
s i t e : 1997 Oletha, Kansas; 1998 Crystal Lake, Illinois

p r o j e c t : **NBC News Broadcast Studio for the 1996 Democratic National Convention ◄**
c l i e n t : NBC News
s i t e : United Center, Chicago, Illinois
t e a m : Mark Dewalt (principal-in-charge), Joe Valerio (design principal), David Rasche (project architect), Jason Hall, WMA Consulting Engineers, Ltd. (m/e/p engineering), TT.CBM Engineers (structural engineering), International Contractors, Inc. (general contractor)
a w a r d s : 1997 AIA Chicago Special Recognition Award for Interior Architecturep h o t o s : Barbara Karant of Karant + Associates, Inc.

p r o j e c t : **Virtual Comfort Chair ◄**
c l i e n t : Knoll International, Inc.
s i t e : Chicago, Illinois

p r o j e c t : **Palm Computing Headquarters, Sales and R&D Facility**
c l i e n t : U.S. Robotics Corporation
s i t e : Mountain View, California
c o m p l e t e d : 1997

p r o j e c t : **Capital Projects Database**
c l i e n t : U.S. Robotics Corporation

p r o j e c t : **Offices for WMA Consulting Engineers, Ltd. ◄**
c l i e n t : WMA Consulting Engineers, Ltd.
s i t e : Chicago, Illinois
c o m p l e t e d : 1996
t e a m : Joe Valerio (principal-in-charge), Neil J. Sheehan (project architect), Kasia Gawlik Parker, Ericka Pagel, Marius Ronnett, Stephen Katz, Nancy Willert (interiors), WMA Consulting Engineers, Ltd (m/e/p engineering), The Loftrium (general contractor)
a w a r d s : 1997 AIA Chicago Honor Award for Interior Architecture; 1997 Record Interiors Award from *Architectural Record*
p h o t o s : Barbara Karant of Karant + Associates, Inc.

p r o j e c t : **Park Pavilion and Park Place Cafe**
c l i e n t : Lincoln Park Zoological Society
s i t e : Lincoln Park Zoo in Chicago, Illinois
c o m p l e t e d : 1998

p r o j e c t : **Remote Sales Offices (various)**
c l i e n t : U.S. Robotics Corporation
s i t e s : 1996 Dallas, Texas; 1996 New York, New York; 1996 Irvine, California; 1996 Denver, Colorado

p r o j e c t : **Remote Sales Offices and R&D Facilities (various)**
c l i e n t : U.S. Robotics Corporation
s i t e s : 1996 Bellevue, WA; 1996 Vienna, Virginia; 1996 Westborough, Missouri; 1997 Grass Valley, California; 1997 Englewood, Colorado

p r o p o s a l : **Plainfield Town Center Design Competition ◄**
c o m p e t i t i o n s p o n s o r : The Village of Plainfield,Plainfield Partners Commercial, LLC and The Plainfield Township Park District
c o m p e t i t i o n a d v i s o r : Design Competition Services, Inc.
s i t e : Plainfield, Illinois
t e a m : Joe Valerio (principal-in-charge), David Jennerjahn, Michael Everts, Randy Mattheis, David Rasche, Neil J. Sheehan, David Dylo, Kasia Gawlik Parker, Jason Hall, Daniel Harmon, Elana Katz, Brian Korte, Brian Maite, Sarah Morie, Brad Pausha, Louis Ray, Rosa Shyn, Heather Wasilowksi, Steve Wilmot
a w a r d s : exhibitor status

p r o j e c t : **Remote Sales Office and R&D Facility**
c l i e n t : 3Com Corporation
s i t e : Denver, Colorado
c o m p l e t e d : 1998

p r o j e c t : **3Com Midwest Corporate Campus ◄**
c l i e n t : 3Com Corporation
s i t e : Rolling Meadows, Illinois
c o m p l e t e d : 1998
t e a m : collaboration with STUDIOS Architecture of San Francisco on the campus master plan. Phase I project design by Valerio Dewalt Train, except for the multi-purpose room, executive briefing center, training center and company store which were designed by STUDIOS. Team members are: Joe Valerio (principal-in-charge), Randy Mattheis (project architect), Ken Wertz, Brad Pausha, Sarah Morie, Daniel Harmon, Rosa Shyn, Jason Hall, Wendy Mingin, Christine

McGrath, Kasia Gawlik Parker, Pamela Crowell, Michael Everts, Kurt Hunt, Dana Sanchez, Heather Salisbury, Mark Cuellar, Brian Maite; Robert Darvas Associates (structural engineers), Nancy Willert (interiors consultant), WMA Consulting Engineers, Ltd. (m/e/p engineering), Gaiatech (environmental engineering), SDI Consultants (civil engineering), Security by Design (security consultants), Cini-Little International (food service consultants), EIS inc. (audio-visual consultants), Don Belford Associates (structural engineering review), Architecture and Light (California lighting consultants), Charter-Sills & Associates (Illinois lighting consultants), Horvath and Associates (curtain wall consultants), Illinois Roof Consulting Associates, Inc. (roof consultants), Metro Transporation Group (traffic consultant), Peter Lindsay Schaudt, L.A. (landscape architecture), Plancom, Inc. (environmental graphics), Professional Club Management (fitness consultant), Shiner + Associates (acoustical consultant), Metropolitan Fire (fire protection), Hill Mechanical Group (mechanical d&b sub), The Boelter Companies (food service d&b sub), Advance Mechanical Systems, Inc. (plumbing d&b sub) Turner Construction Co. (general contractor).
p h o t o s : Barbara Karant of Karant + Associates, Inc. and Bruce Van Inwegen

p r o j e c t : **Chicago Area Master Plan**
c l i e n t : 3Com Corporation

p r o j e c t : **Chicago Disposition Study: Manufacturing Consolidation**
c l i e n t : 3Com Corporation

1998
p r o j e c t : **Glenview Child Development Center**
c l i e n t : Village of Glenview and the U.S. Navy
s i t e : Glenview, Illinois

p r o j e c t : **Hawthorne Lane Restaurant Renovation**
c l i e n t : David and Annie Gingrass
s i t e : San Francisco, California
c o m p l e t e d : 1998

p r o j e c t : **Lincoln Park Zoo Main Store and Rooftop Cafe**◄
c l i e n t : Lincoln Park Zoological Society
s i t e : Lincoln Park Zoo in Chicago, Illinois
c o m p l e t e d : 1999 (projected)
t e a m : Joe Valerio (principal-in-charge), Neil J. Sheehan (project architect), Ericka Pagel, Mark Cuellar, Wendy Mingin, Dave Perez, Heather Salisbury, Rosa Shyn, Brian Korte, Kim Frutiger, Michael Flath, WMA Consulting Engineers, Ltd. (m/e/p engineering), SDI Consultants (civil engineering), Jacobs Ryan Associates (landscape architecture), John MacManus Associates (site planning), The Levy Restaurants (food service consultants), AAD (retail design consultants), Don Belford (structural engineering), Turner Construction Company SPD (general contractor)
p h o t o s : Orlando Cabanban Photography

p r o j e c t : **Ohio House Addition** ◄
c l i e n t : Joe Valerio and Linda Searl
s i t e : Chicago, Illinois
c o m p l e t e d : 1999
t e a m : Joe Valerio with Linda Searl, Robert Darvas Associates (structural engineering)
p h o t o s : Orlando Cabanban Photography

p r o j e c t : **3Com Manufacturing Consolidation**
c l i e n t : 3Com Corporation
s i t e : Mount Prospect, Illinois
c o m p l e t e d : 1998

p h o t o g r a p h y

All photos by Barbara Karant of Karant + Associates, Inc., except:

pg. 11: see credit below image
pg. 12: Joe Valerio
pg. 16: see credit below image
pg. 26: Orlando Cabanban Photography
pg. 28: James Steinkamp of Steinkamp/Ballogg Chicago
pg. 32: see credit below image
pg. 43: Joe Valerio
pg. 46: Orlando Cabanban Photography
pg. 47: see credit below image
pg. 61: Joe Valerio
pg. 62: see credit below image
pg. 76: Vincent James
pg. 80: see credit below image
pg. 90: David Jennerjahn
pg. 91: Randy Mattheis and Joe Valerio
pg. 96: see credit below image
pgs. 106 and 109: Joe De Maio of De Maio Photography
pg. 110: Larry W. Schwarm
pg. 111: Joe Valerio
pg. 114: Tim Schermerhorn of the Schermerhorn Group LLC, photo courtesy of Kimball International
pg. 123 and 124 (top left image): Alan Blakely of Alan Blakely Photography
pg. 125: Joe Valerio
pg. 126: Joe Valerio
pg. 141 (two top images): Bruce Van Inwegen
pgs. 150-151: Stuart-Rodgers, Ltd. Photography